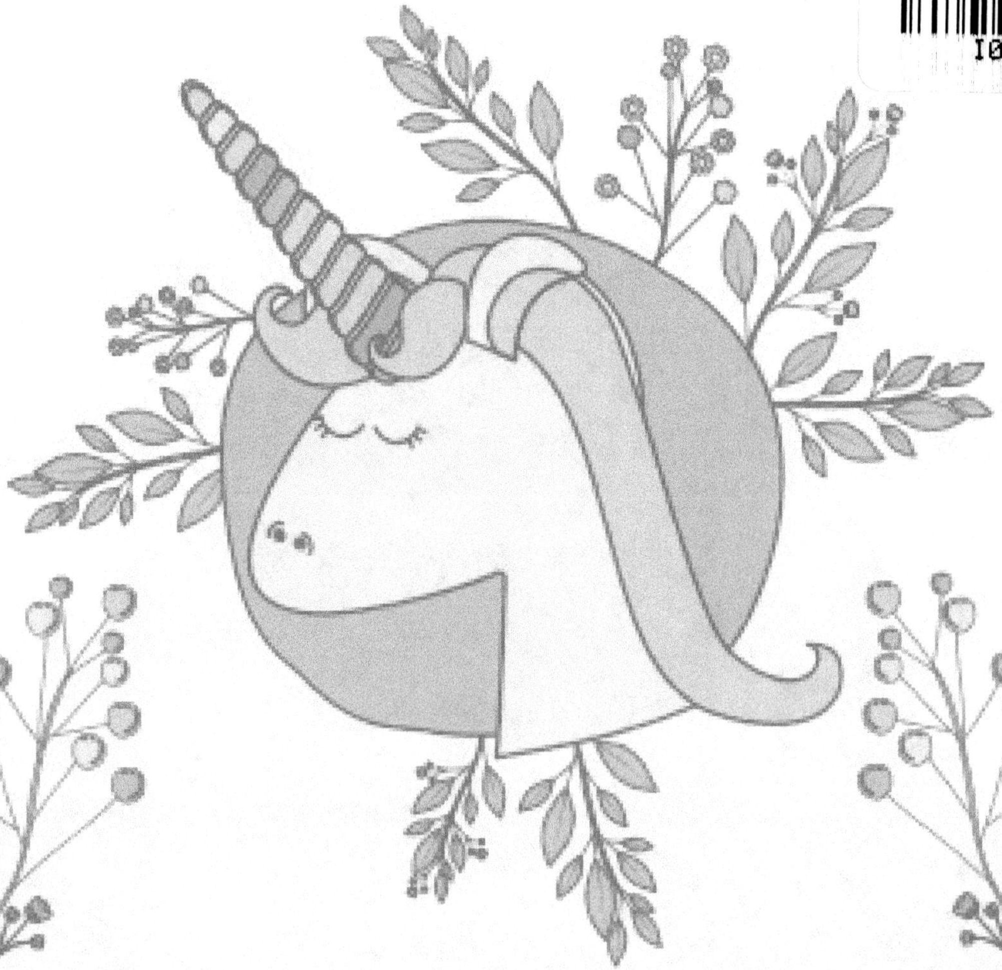

THIS BOOK BELONGS TO

____

Color me!

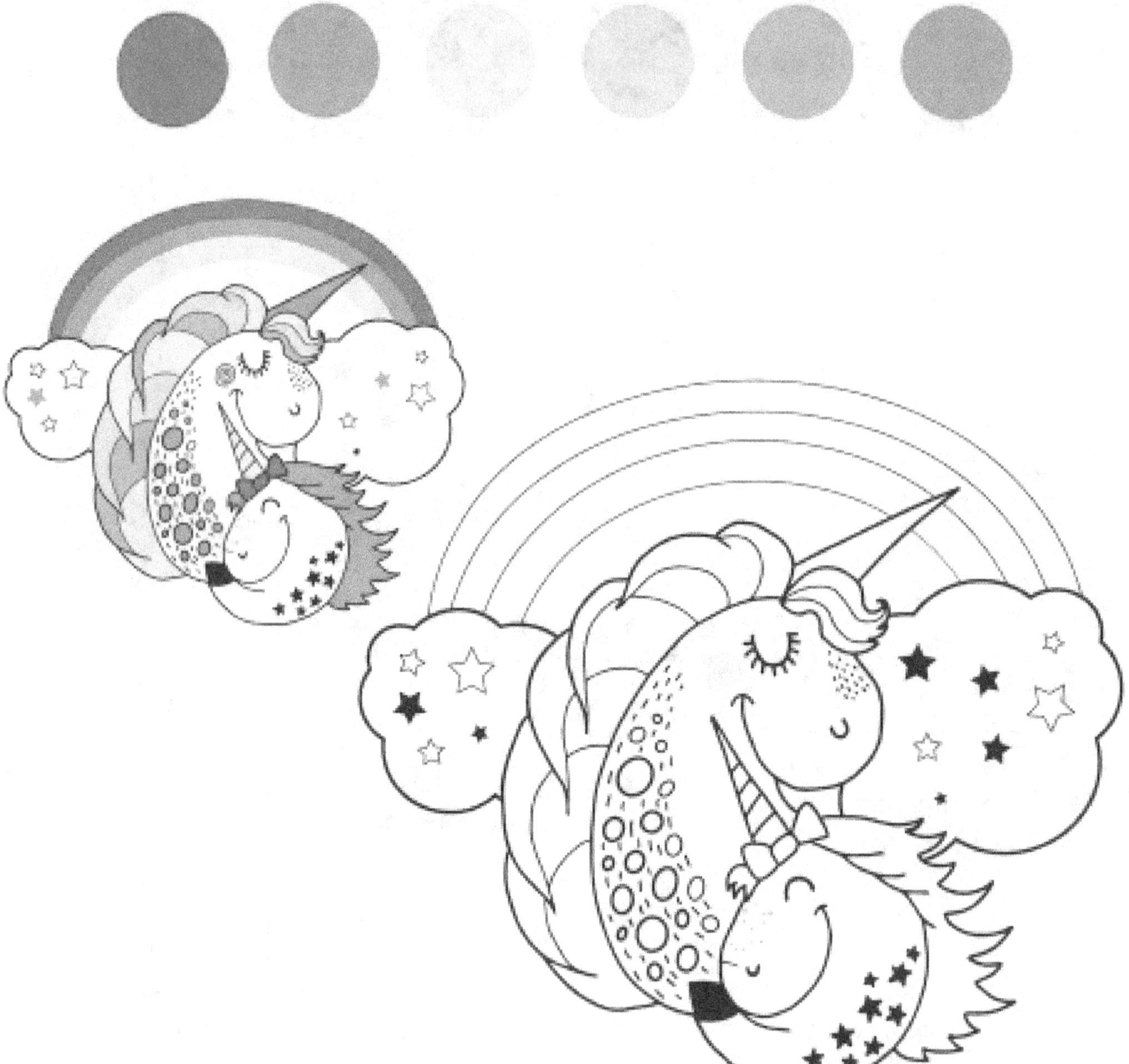

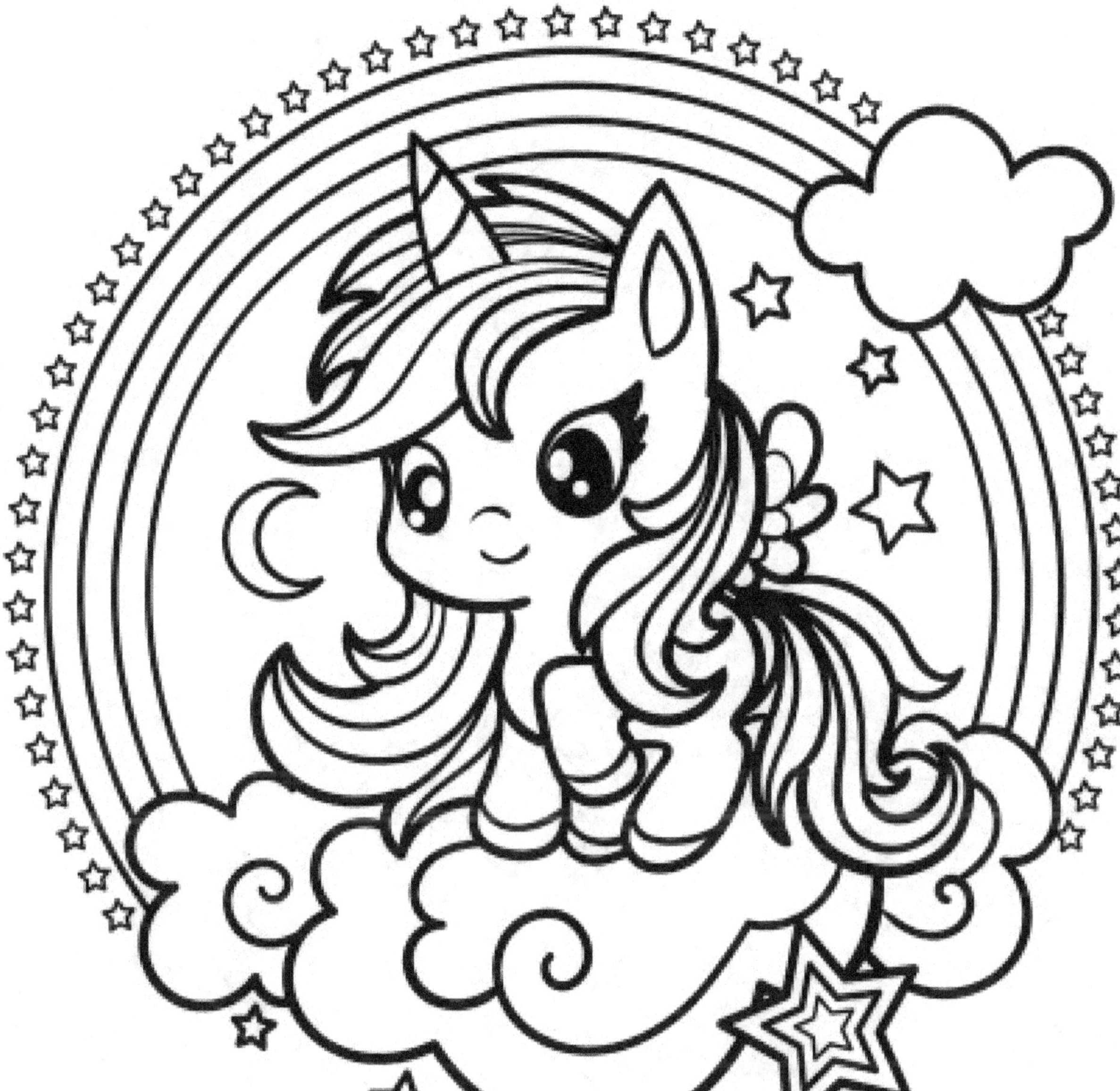

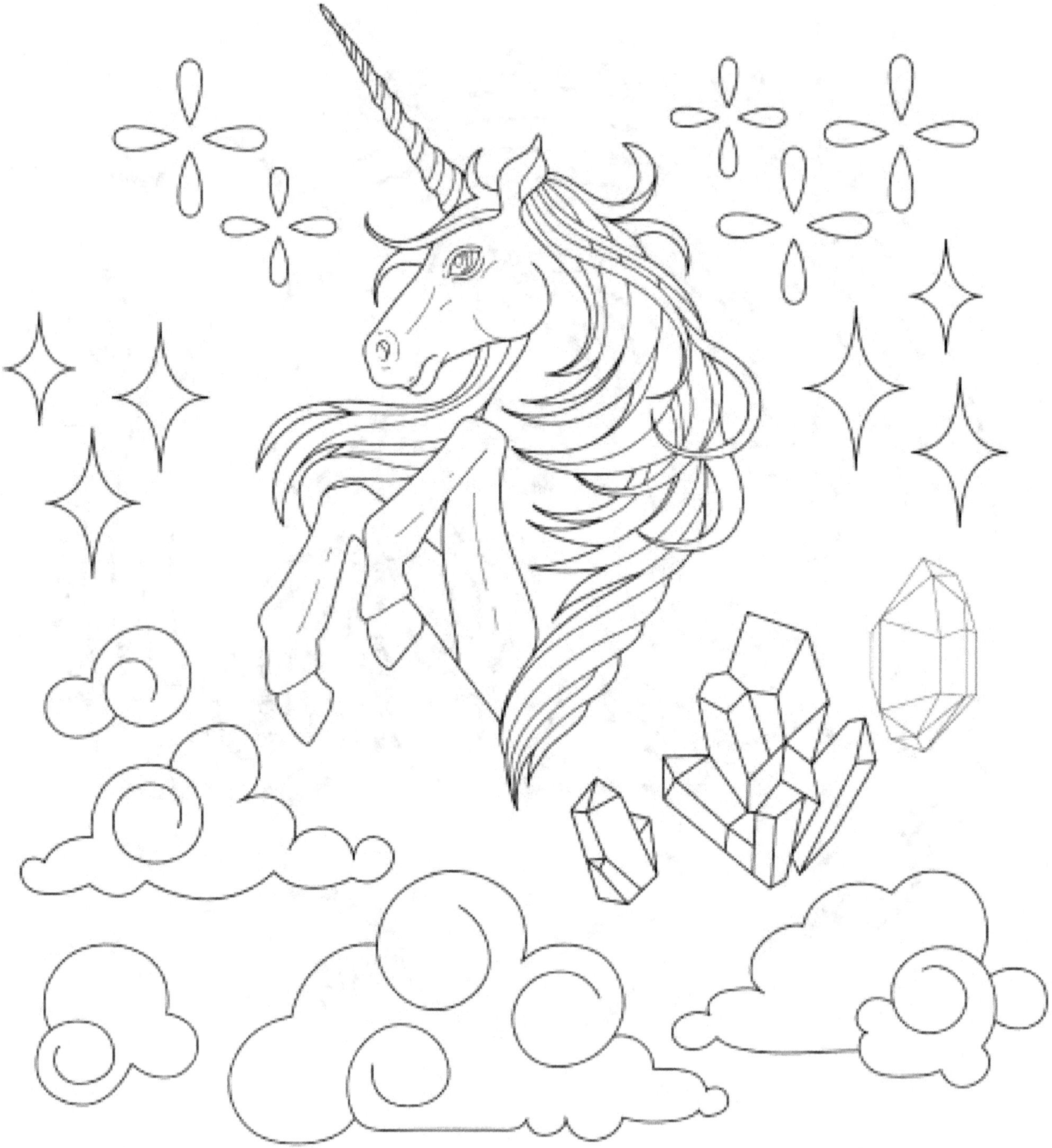

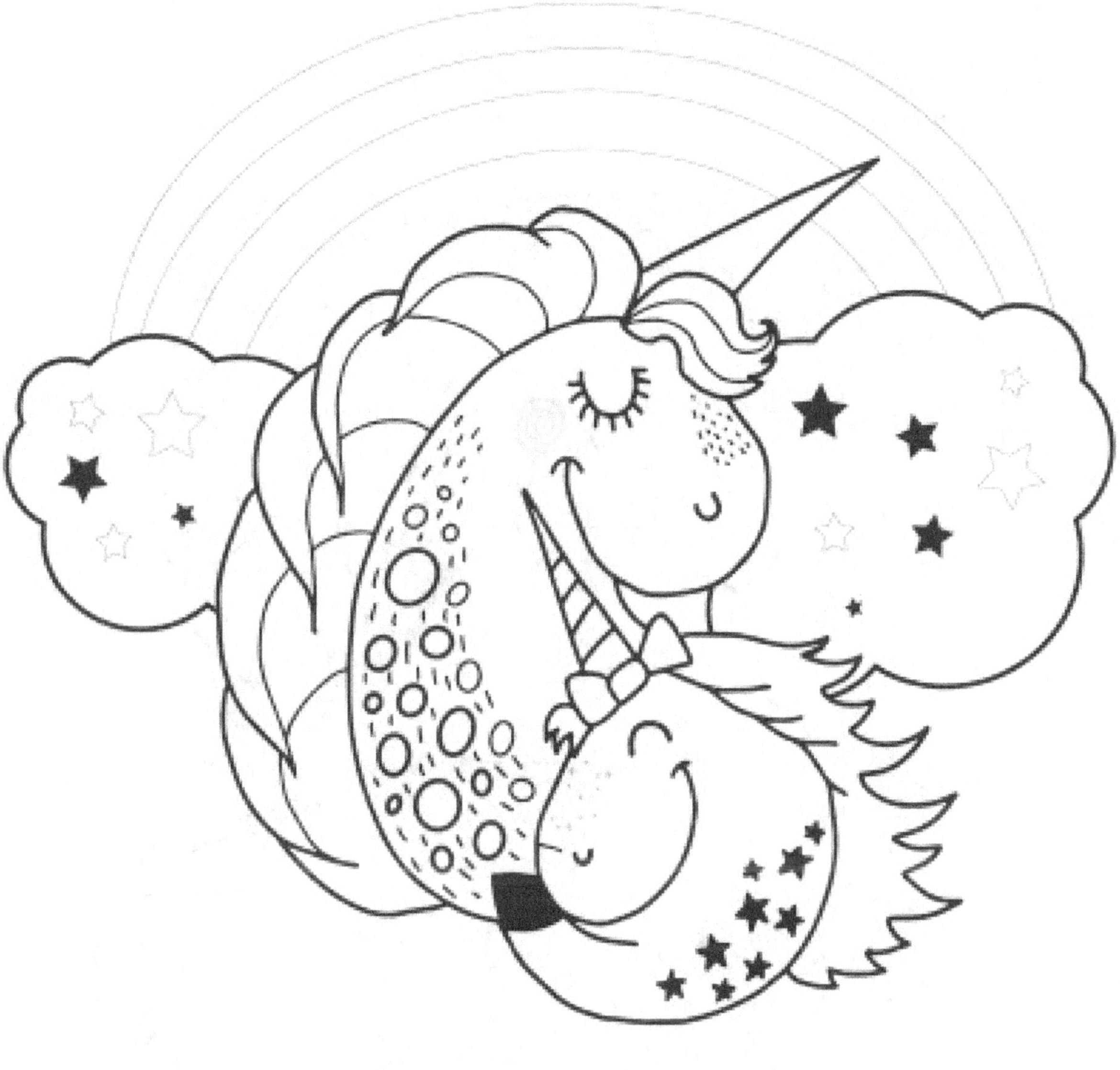

MAGIC

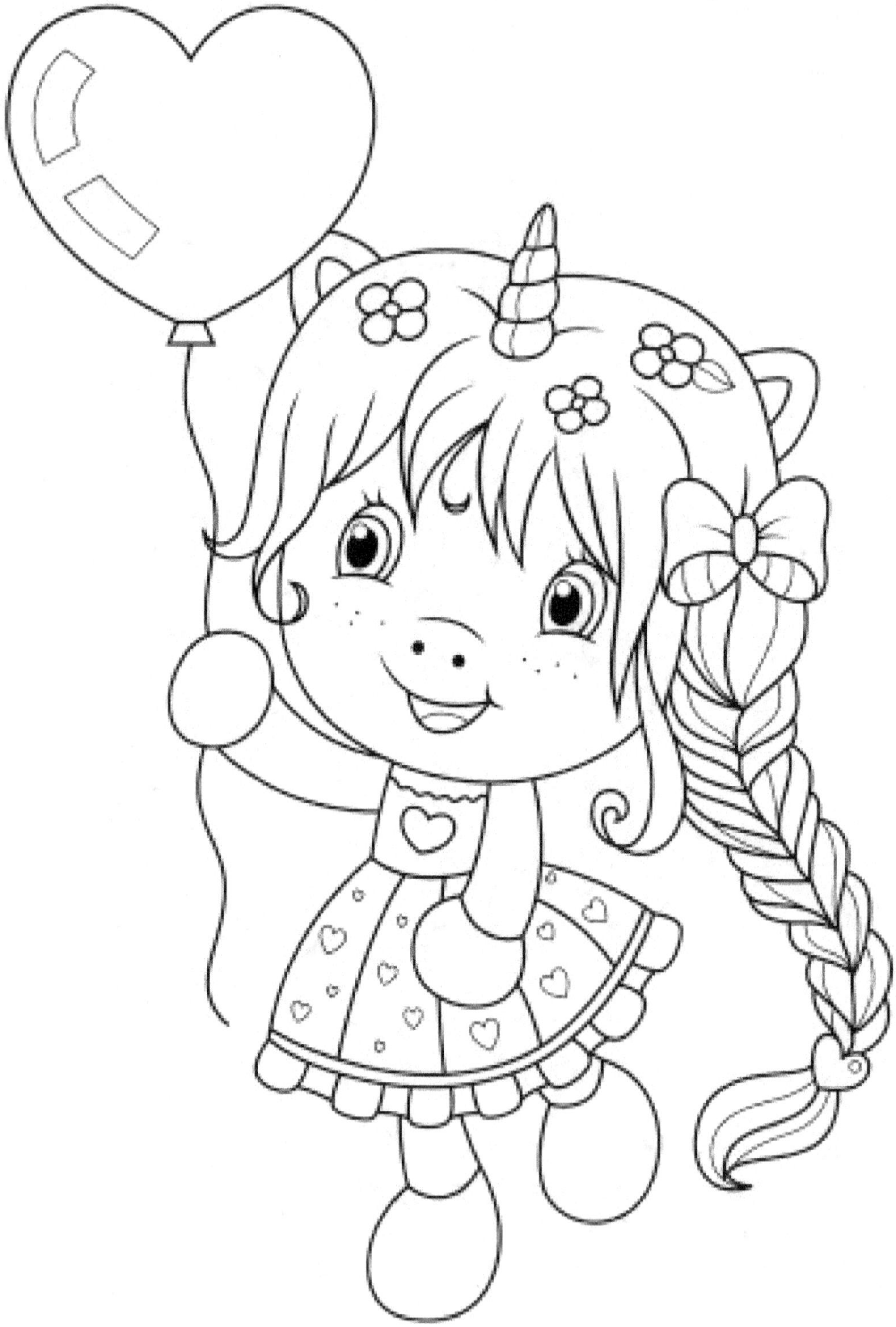

UNICORN

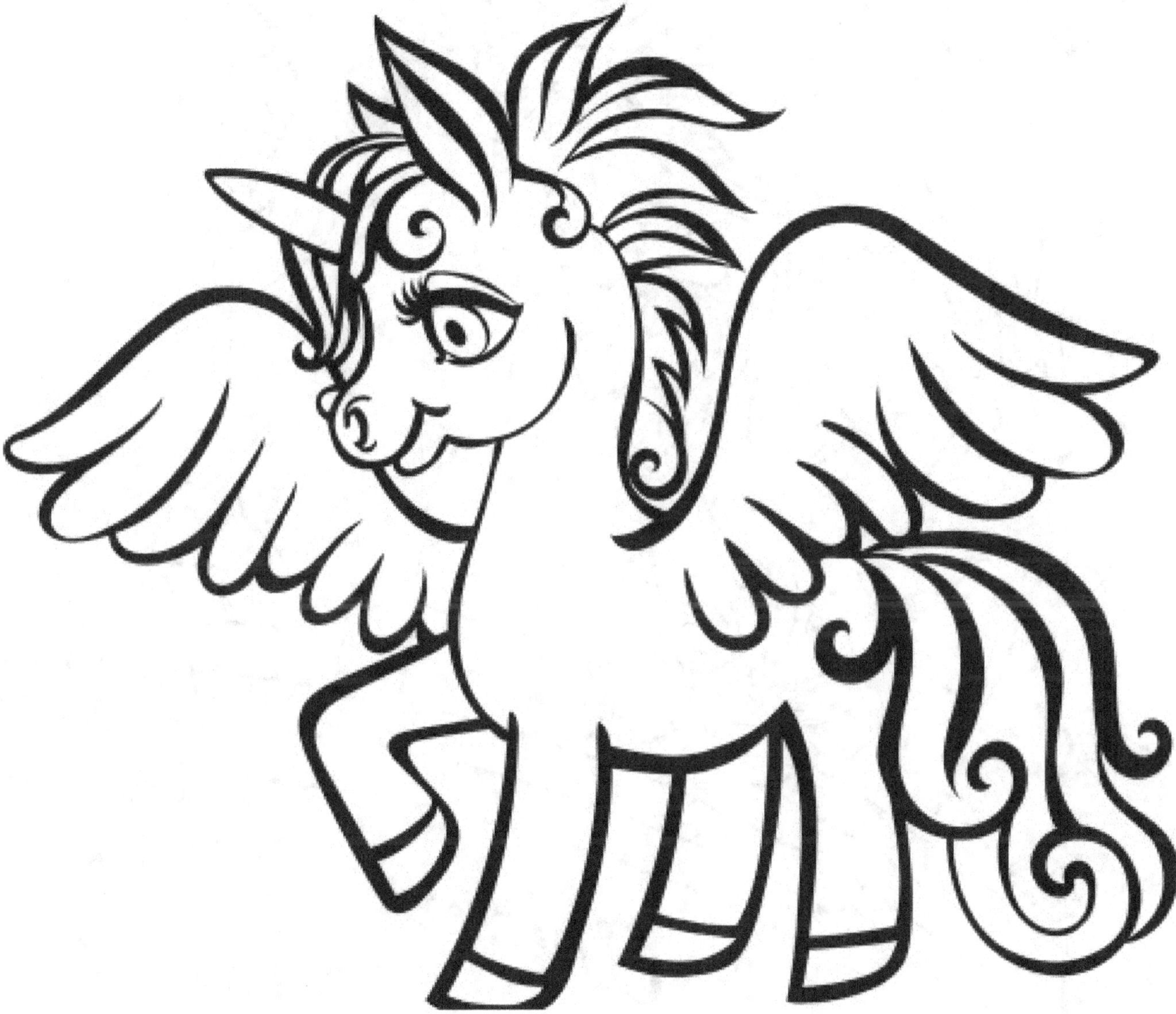

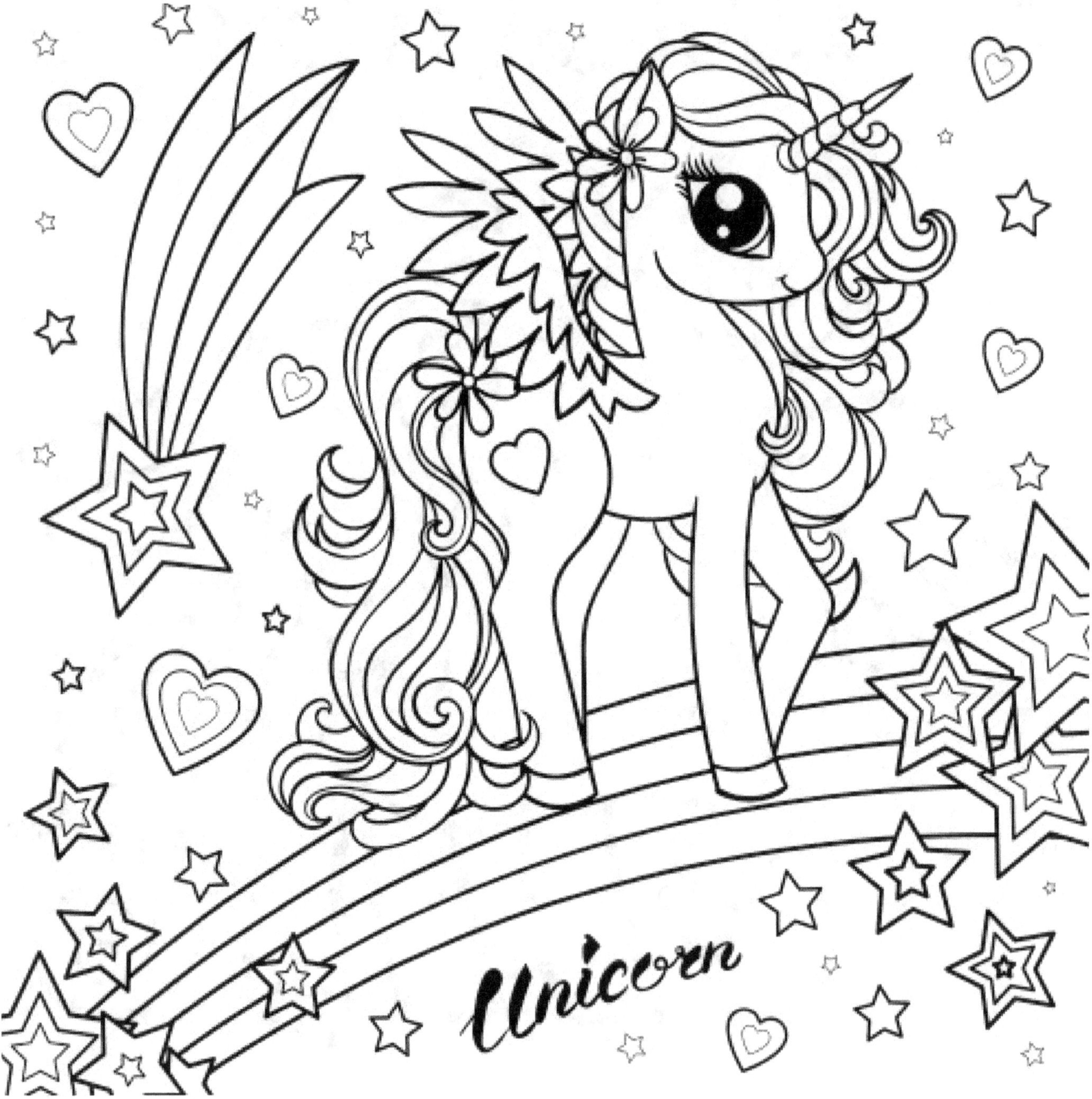
Unicorn

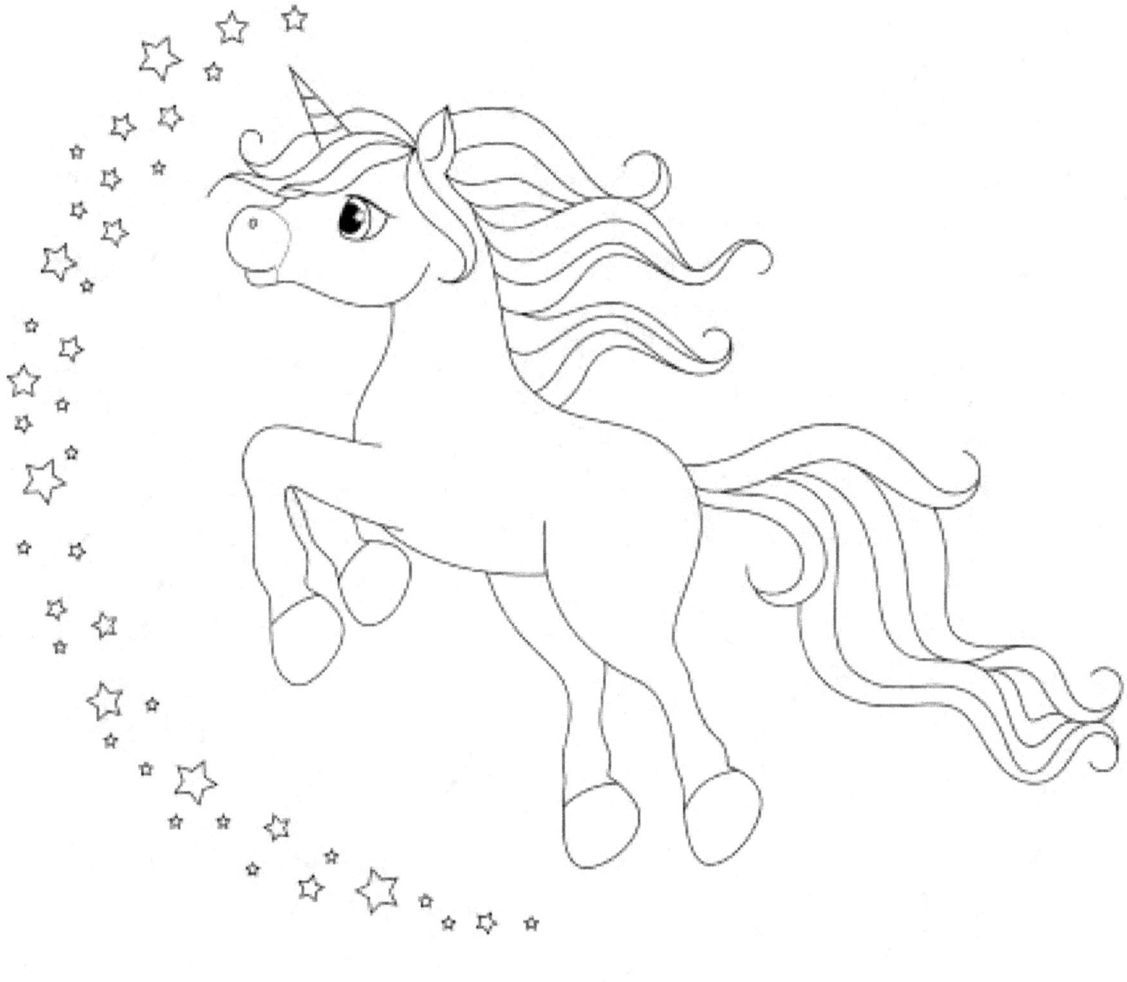

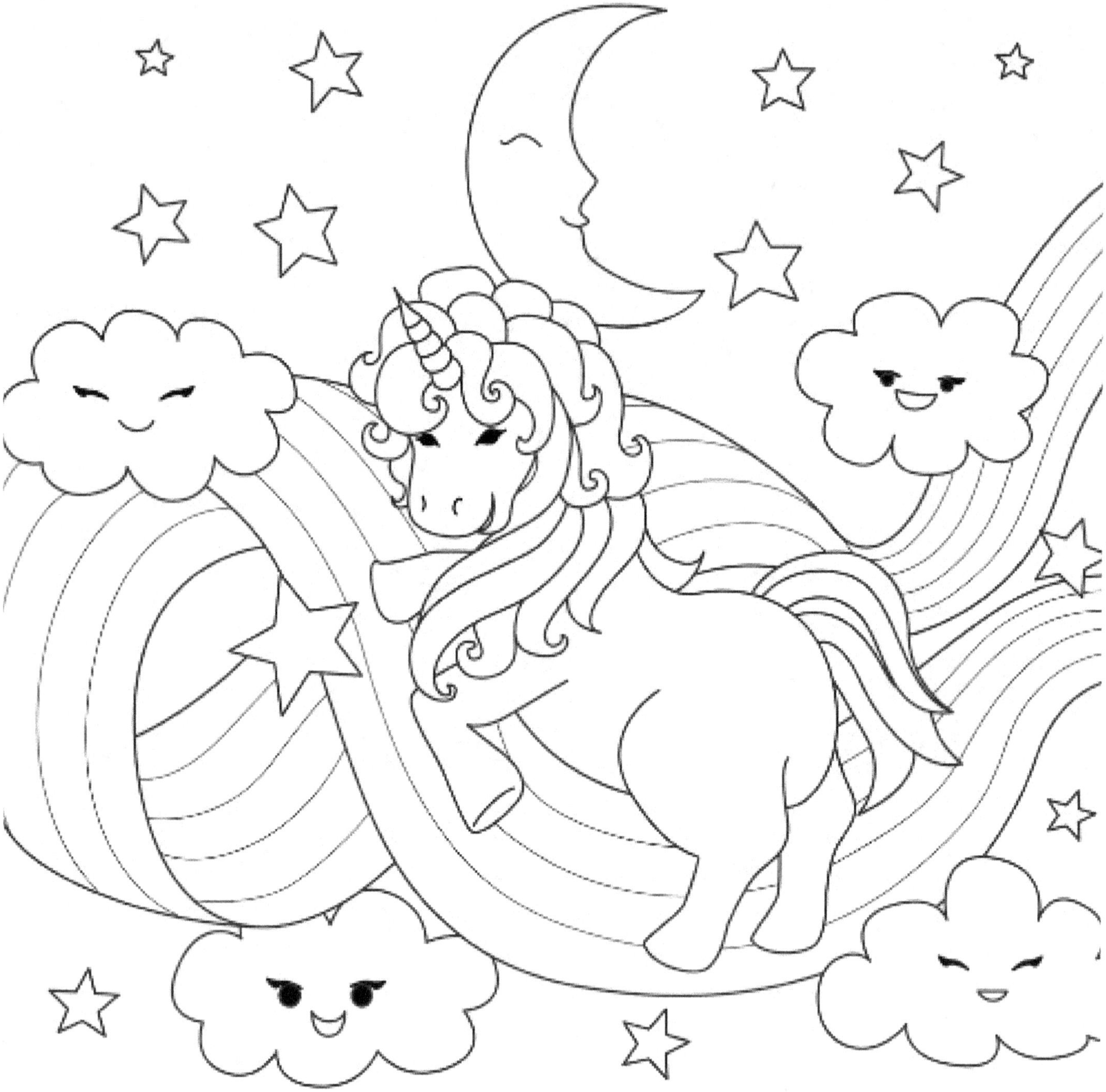

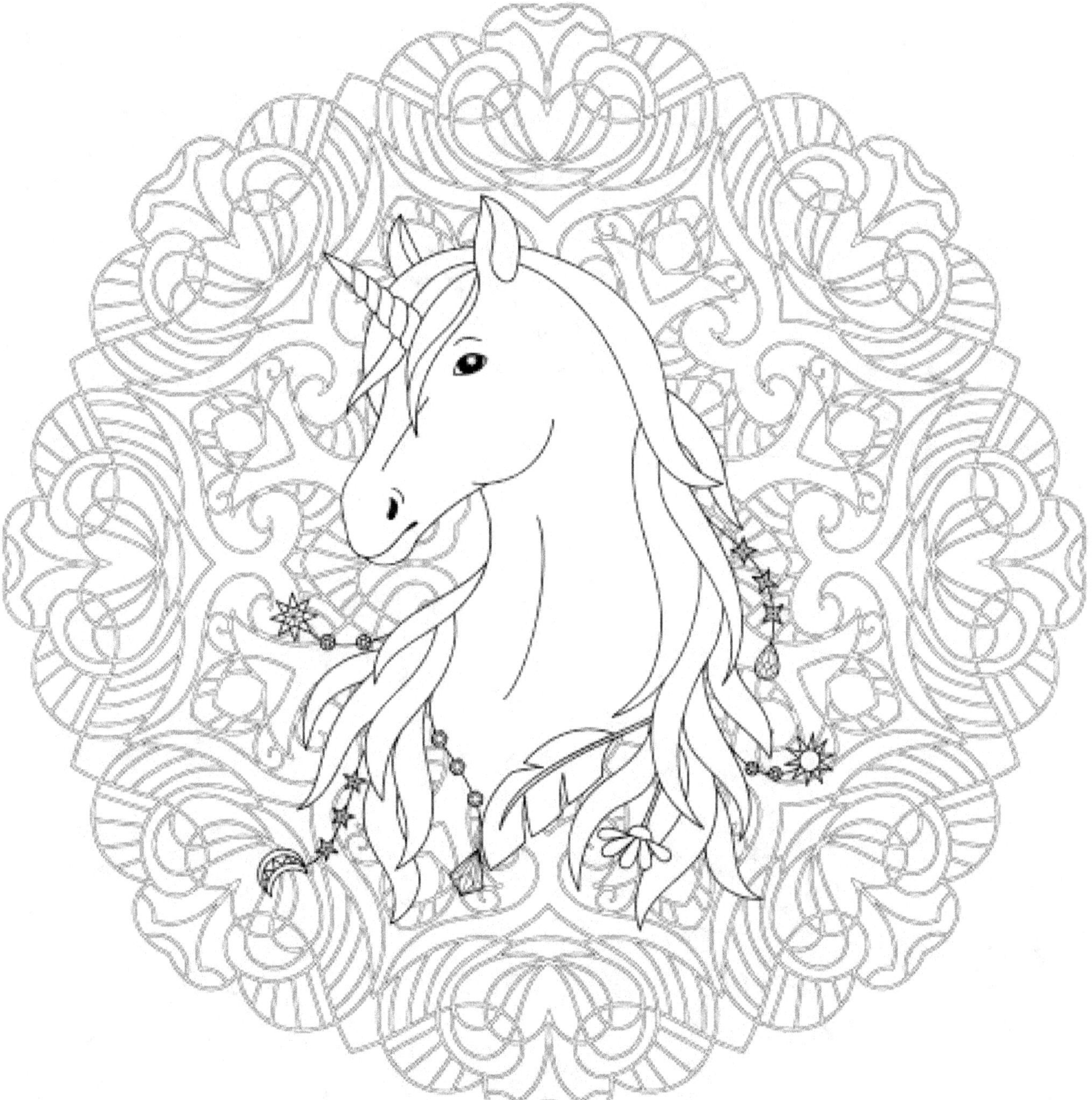

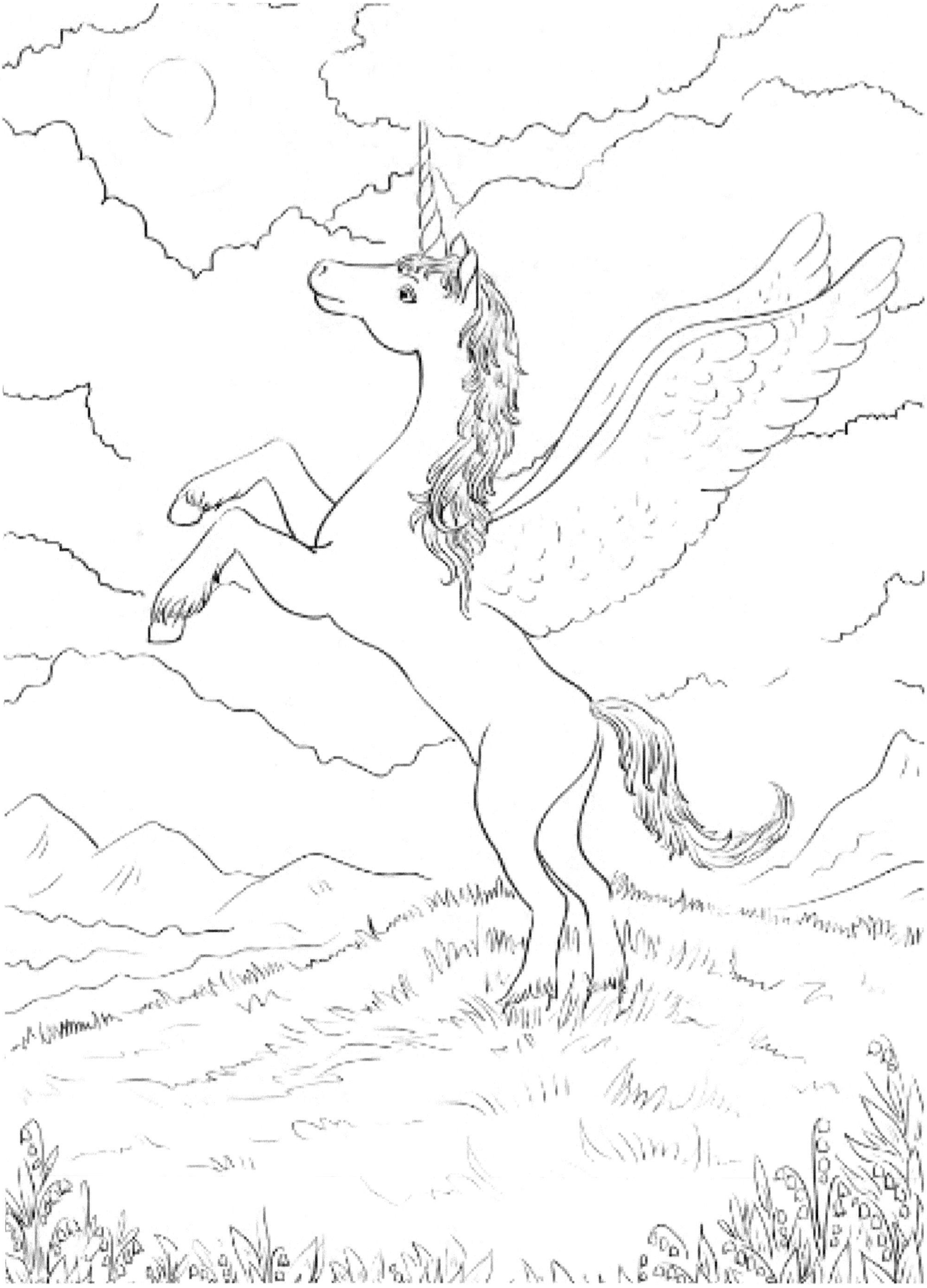

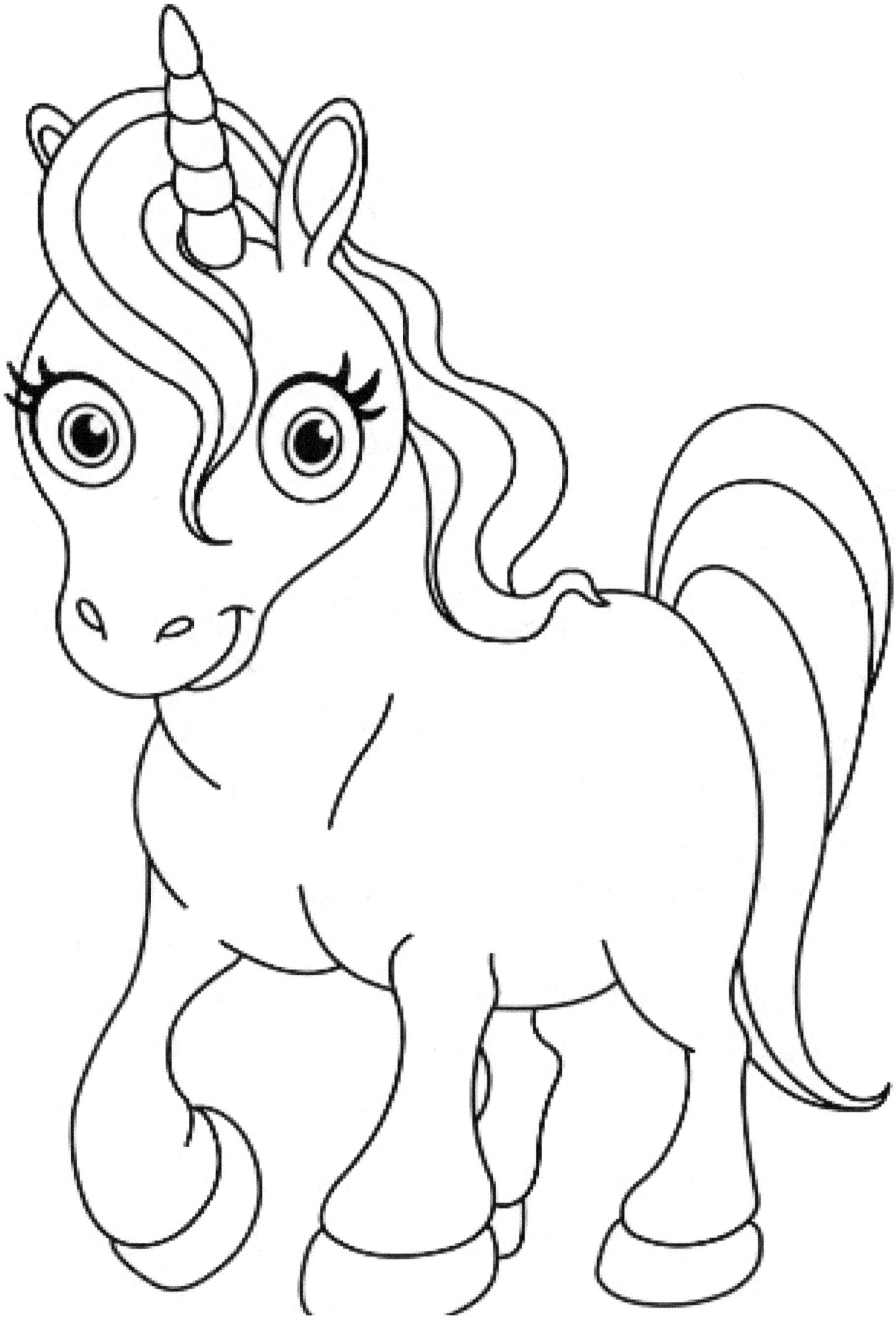

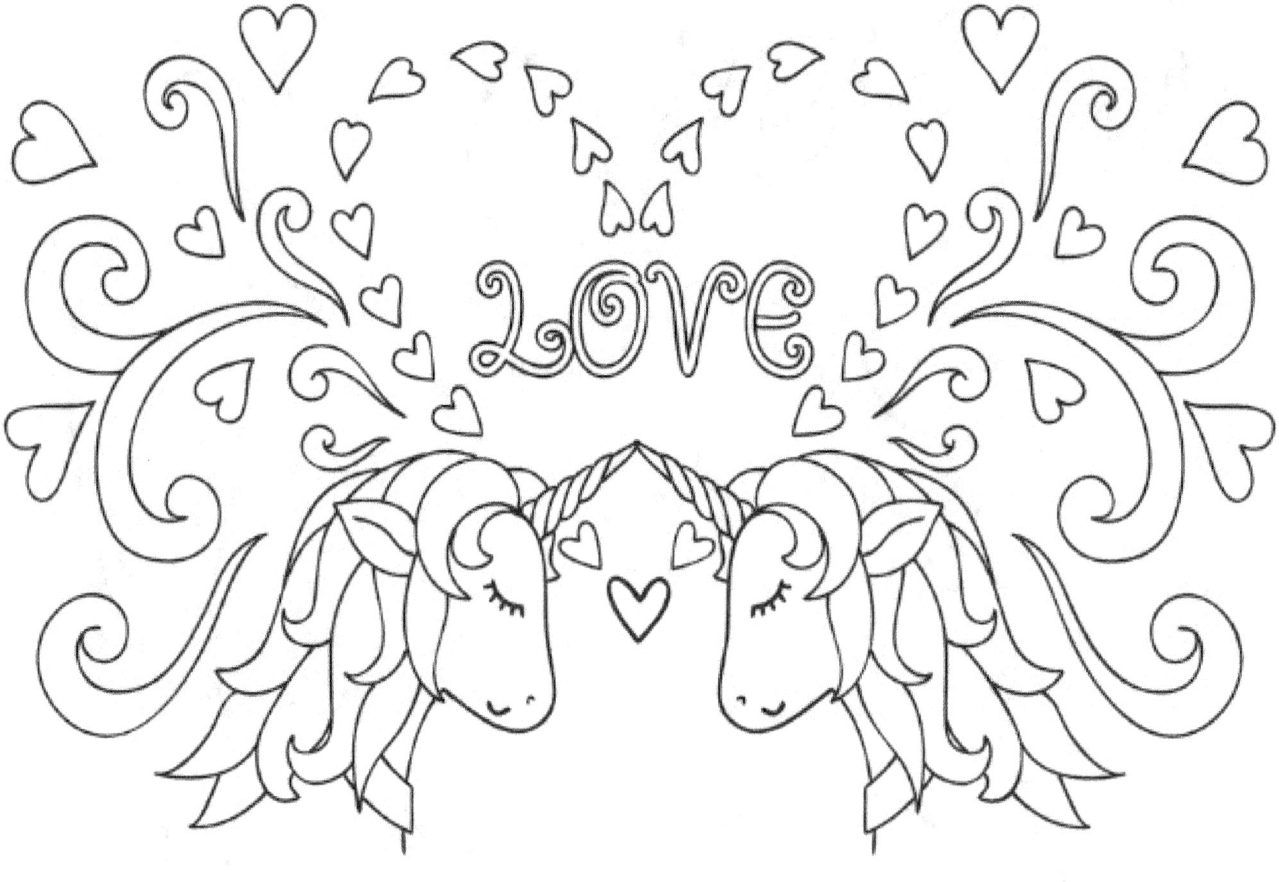
LOVE

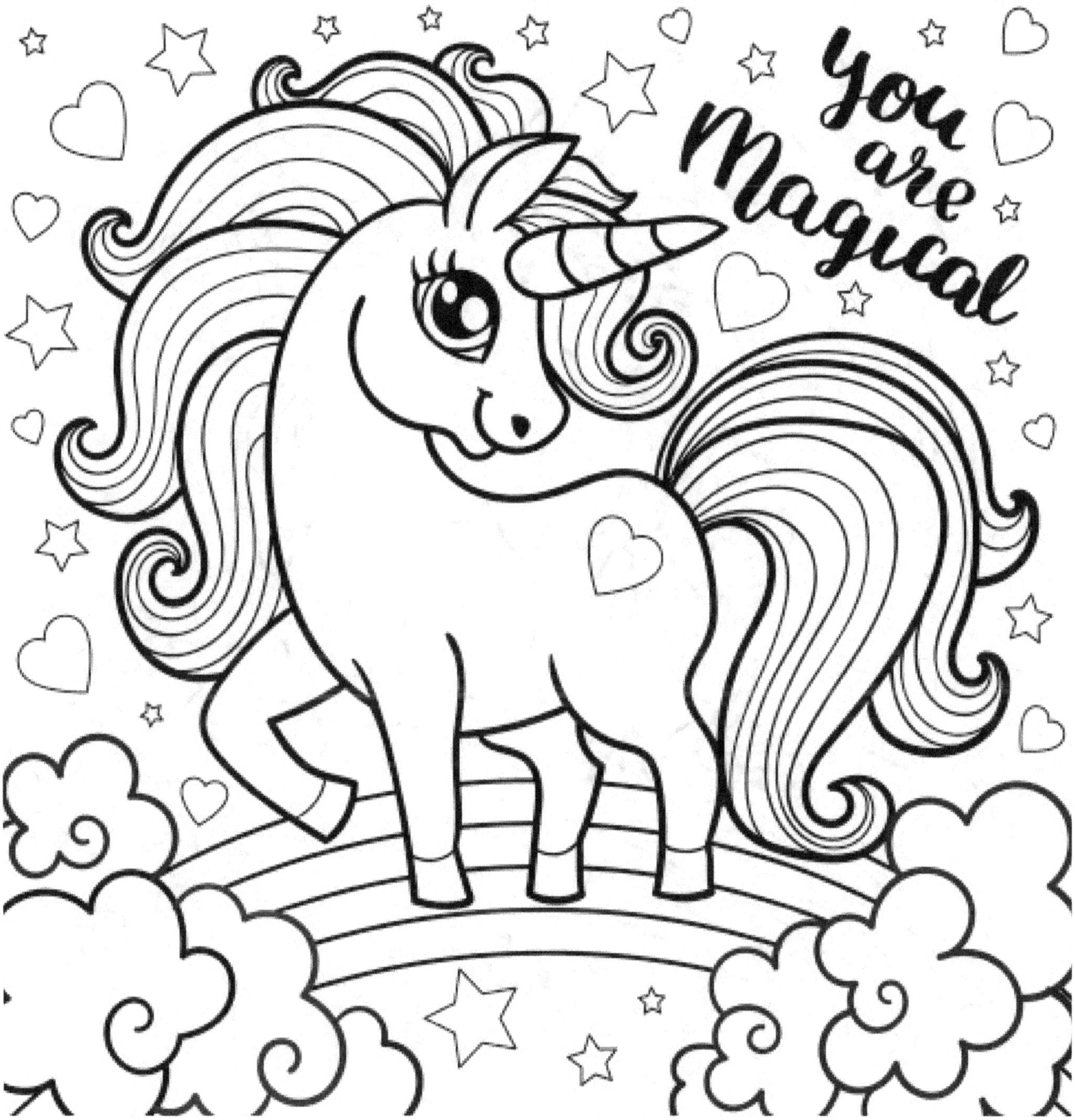
You are Magical

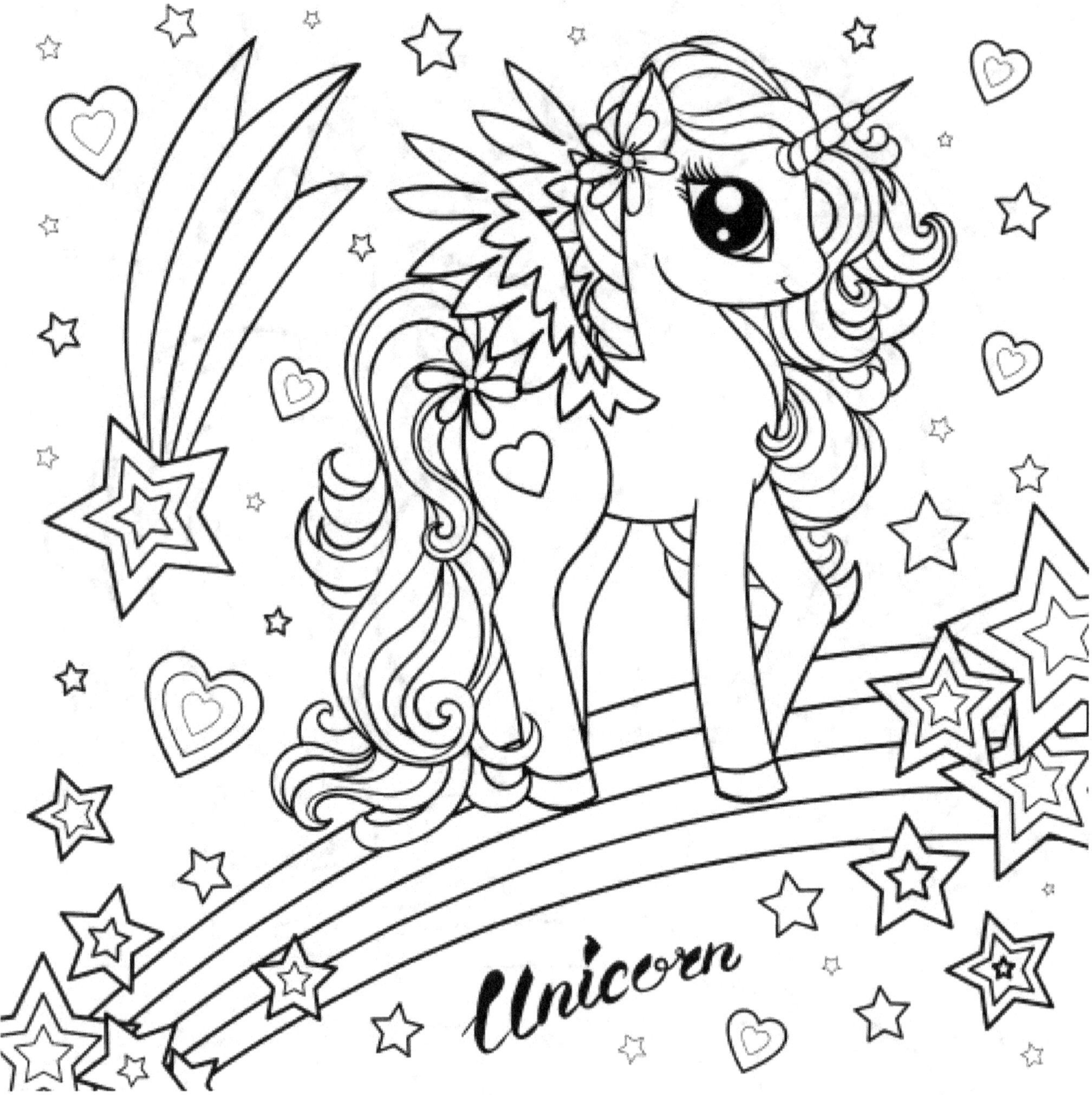
Unicorn

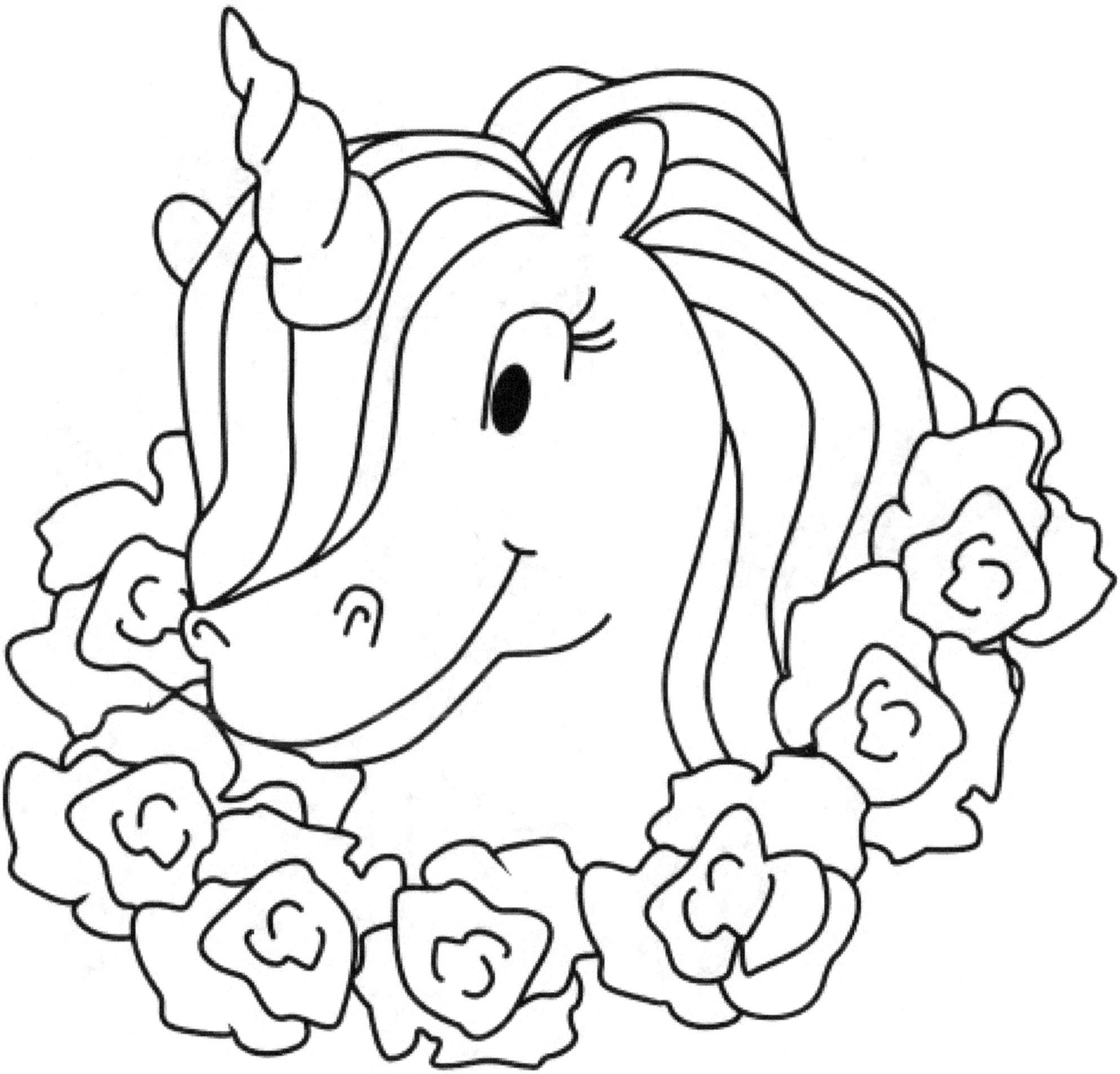

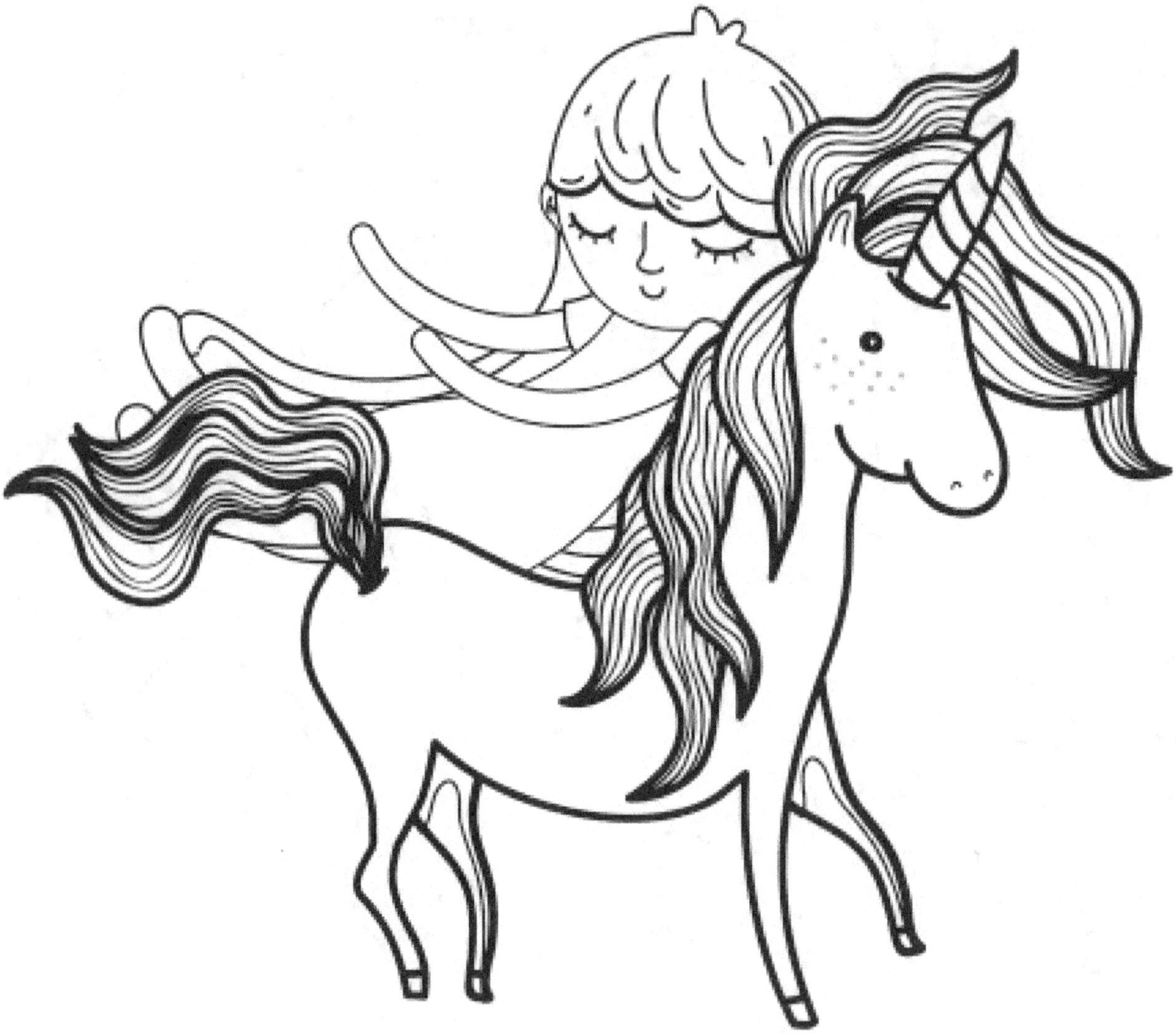

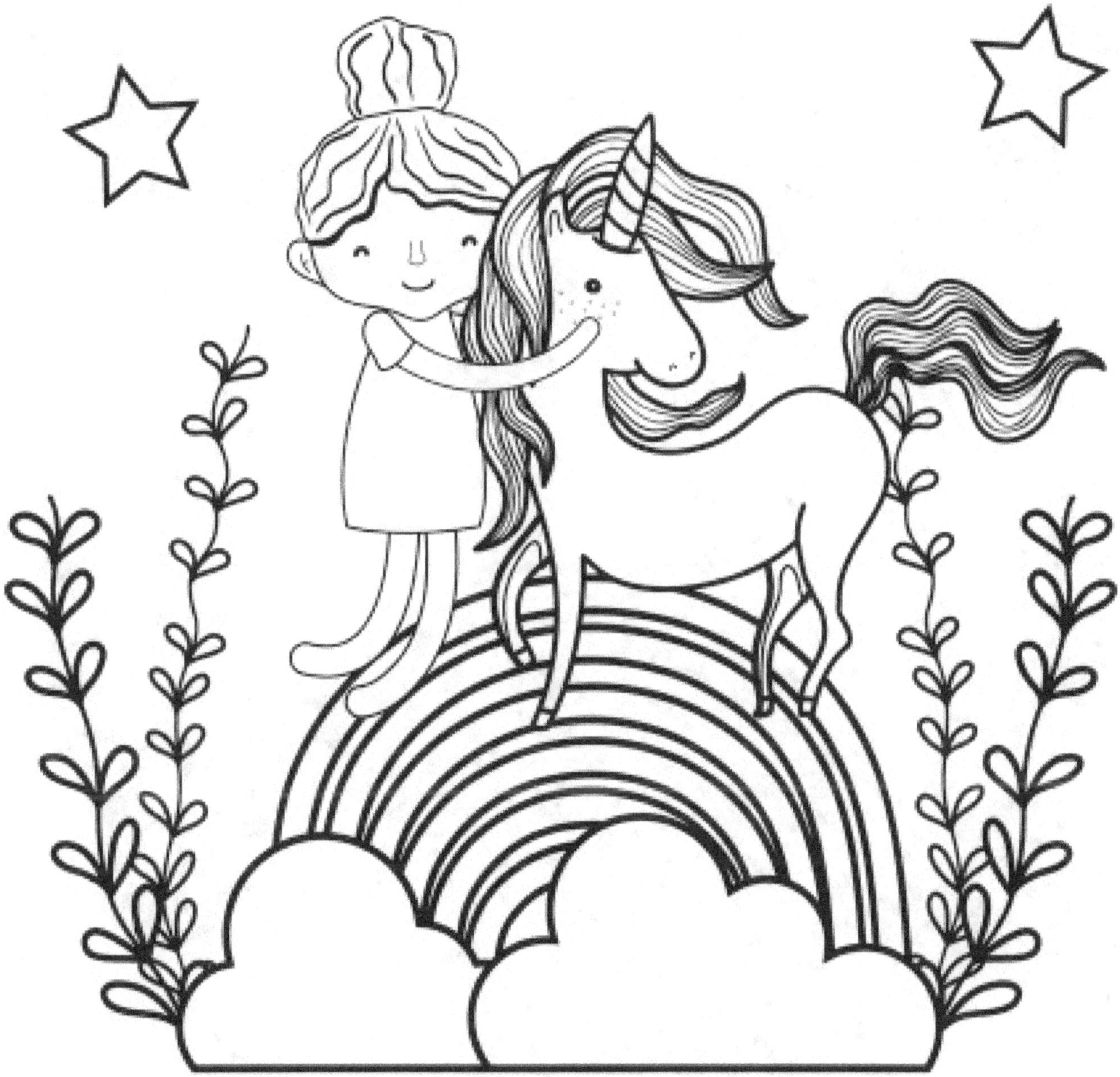

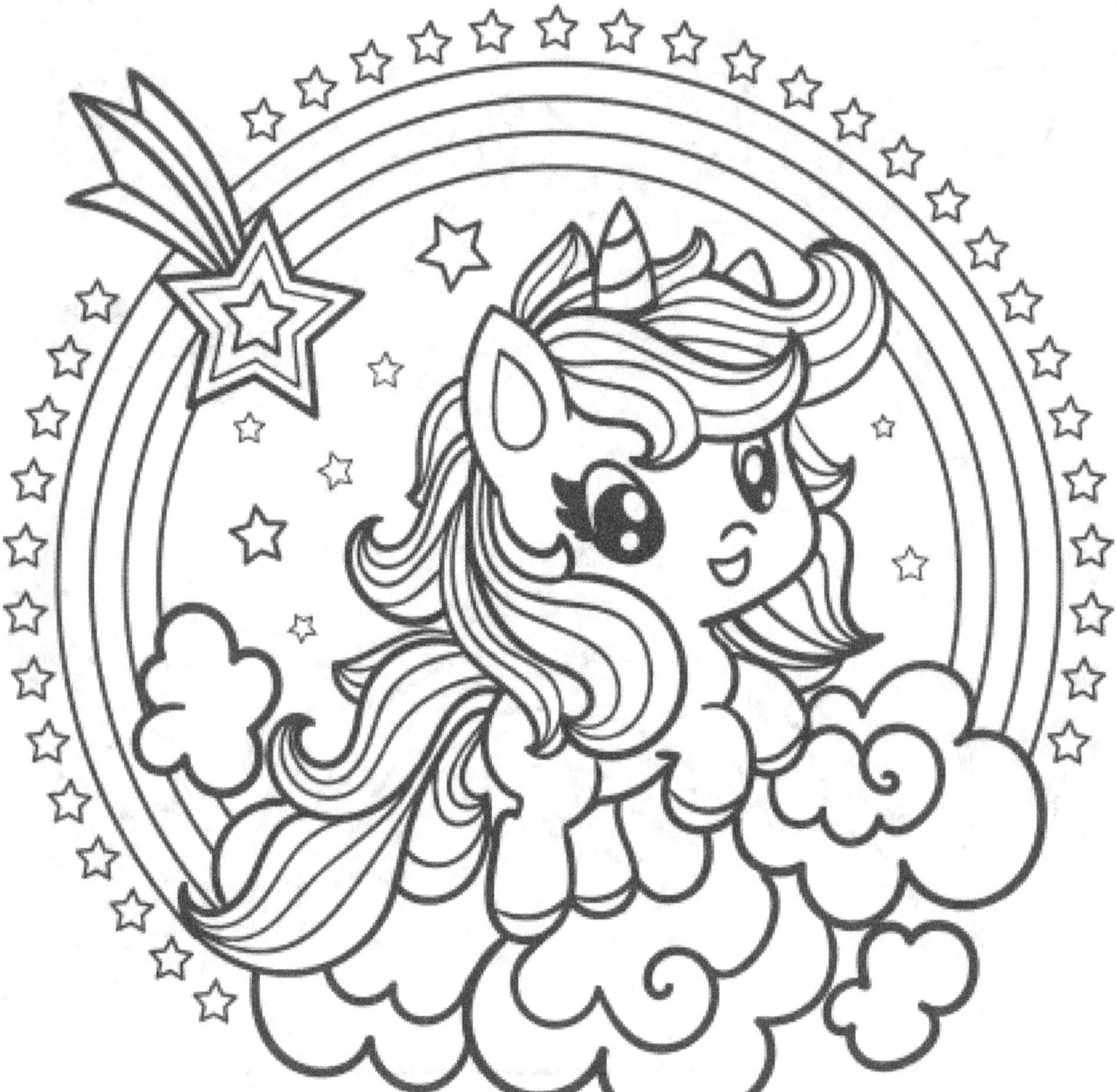

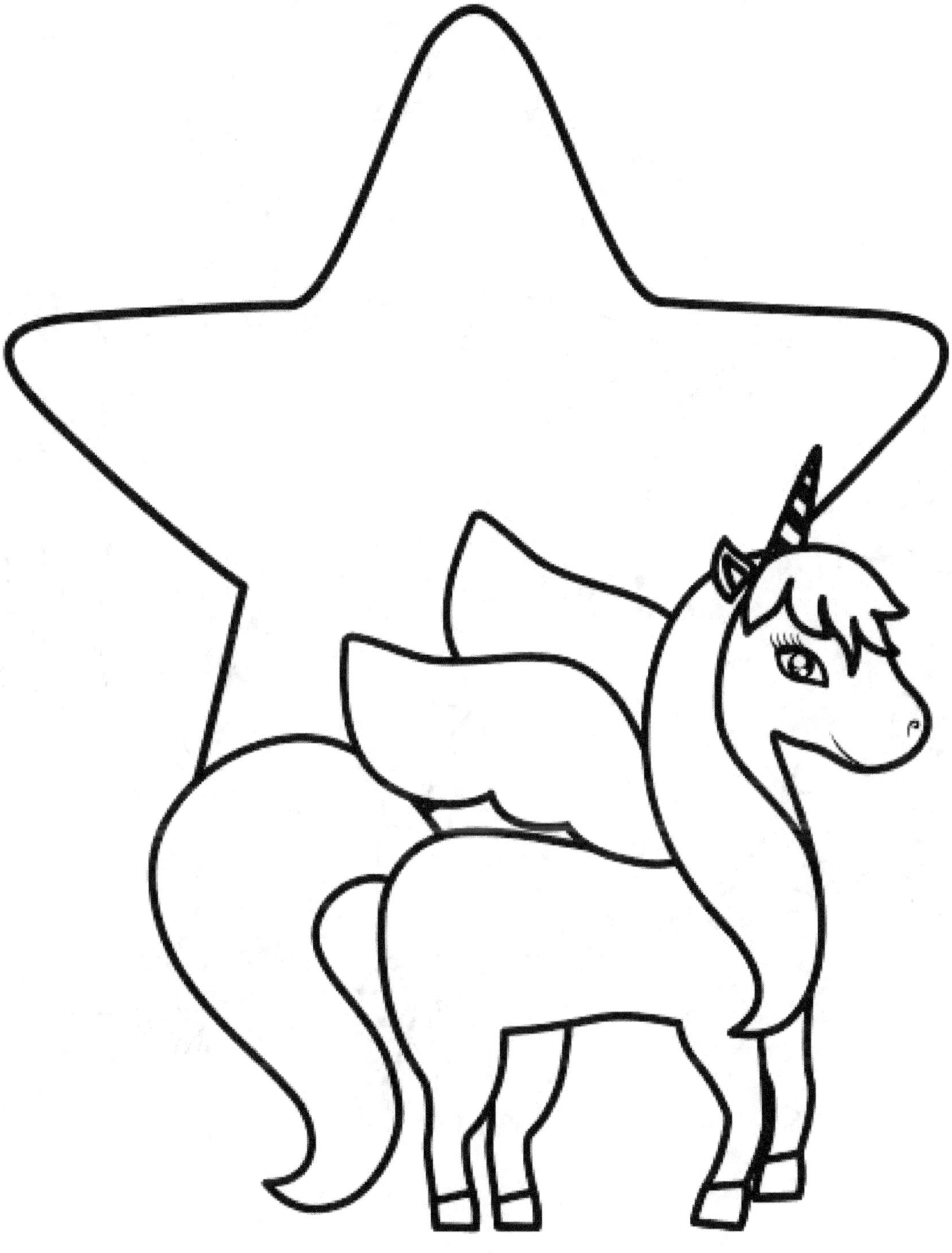

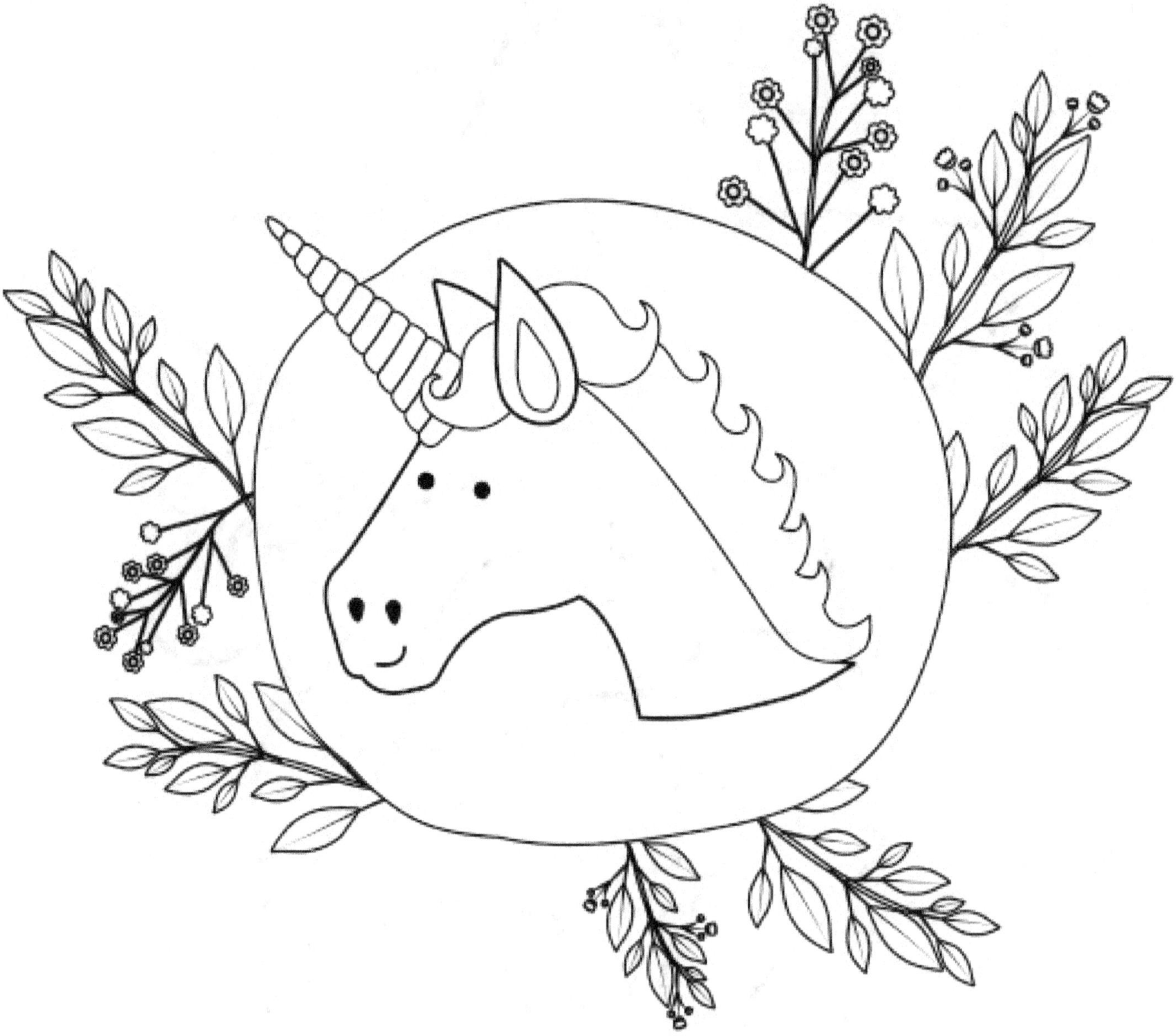

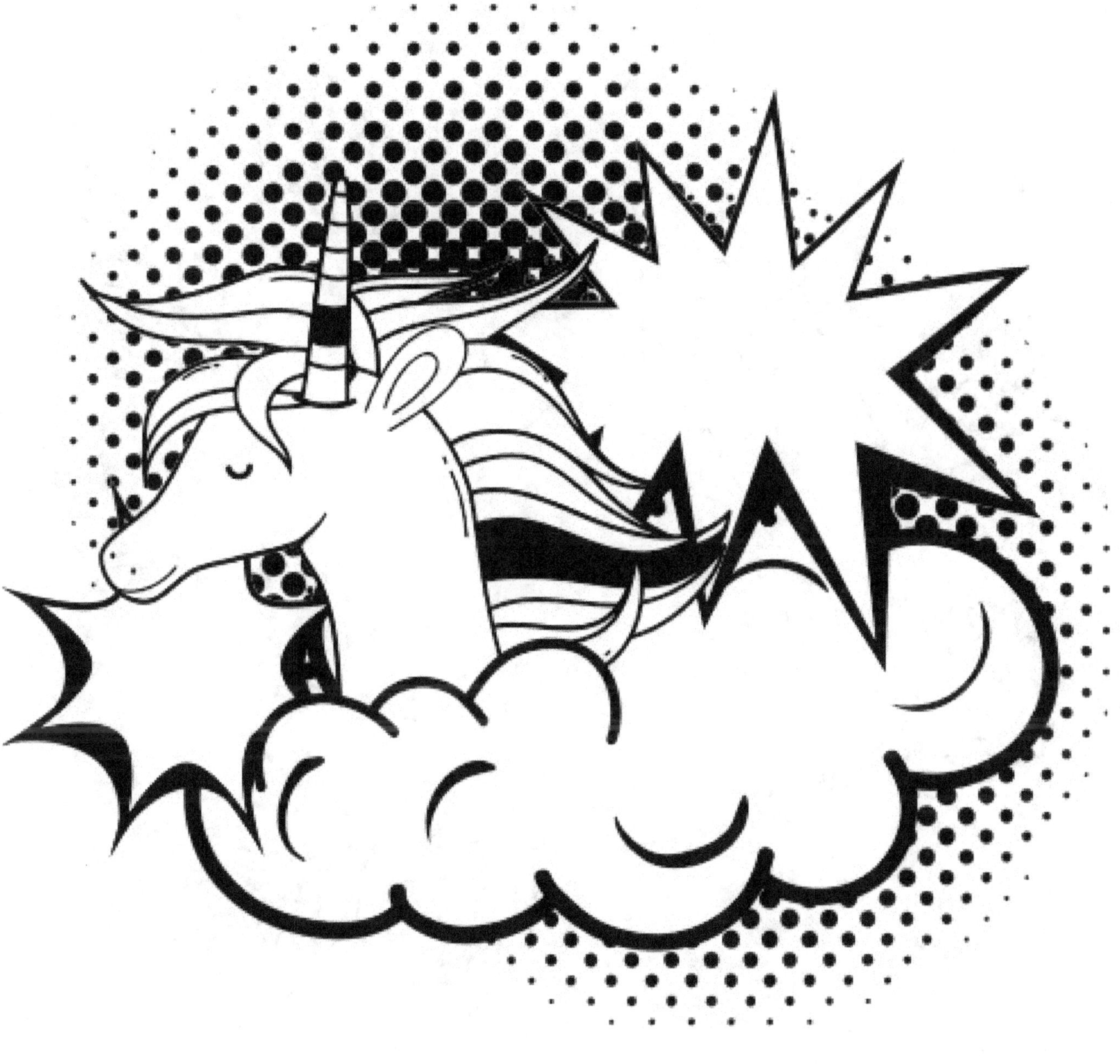

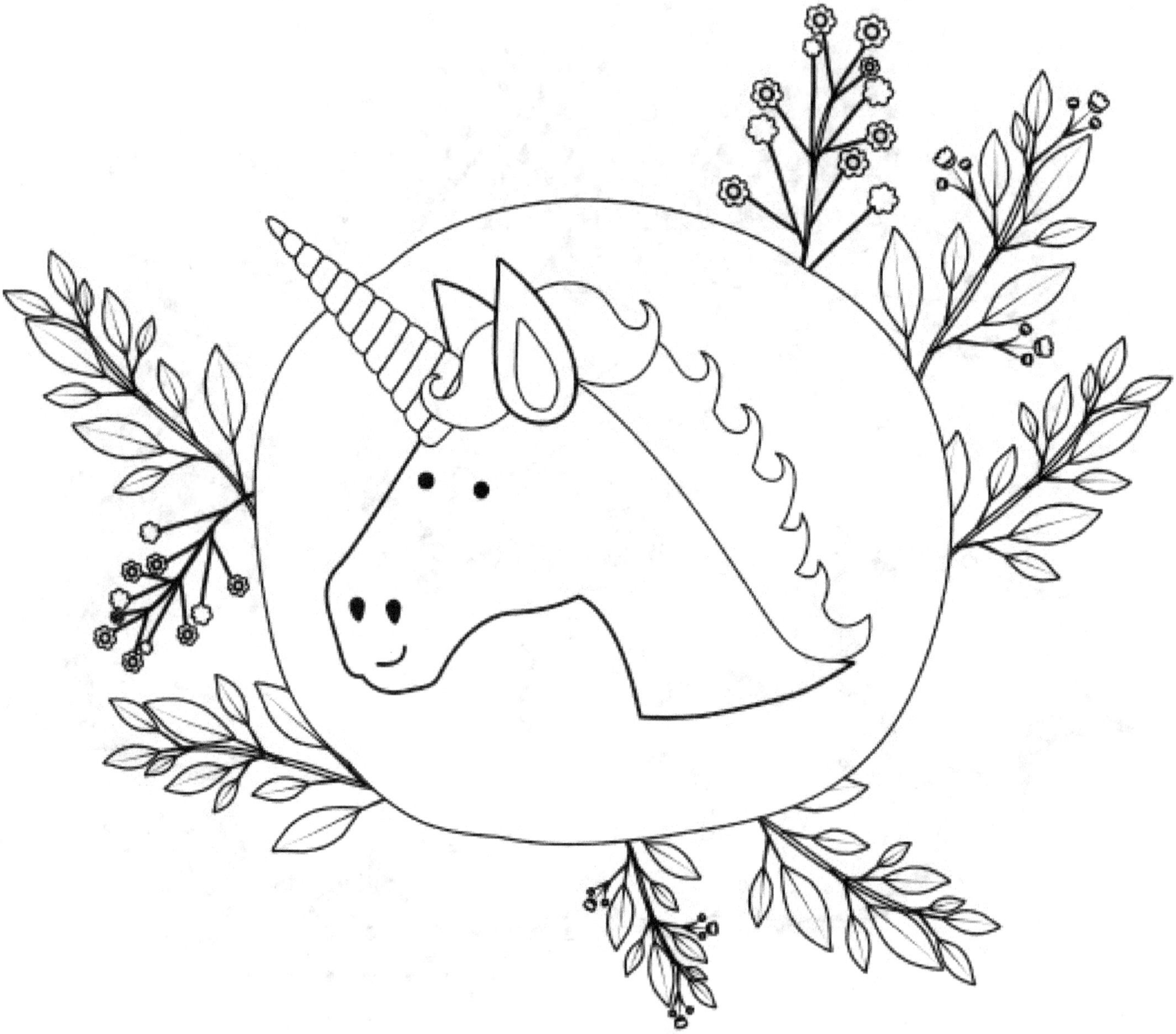

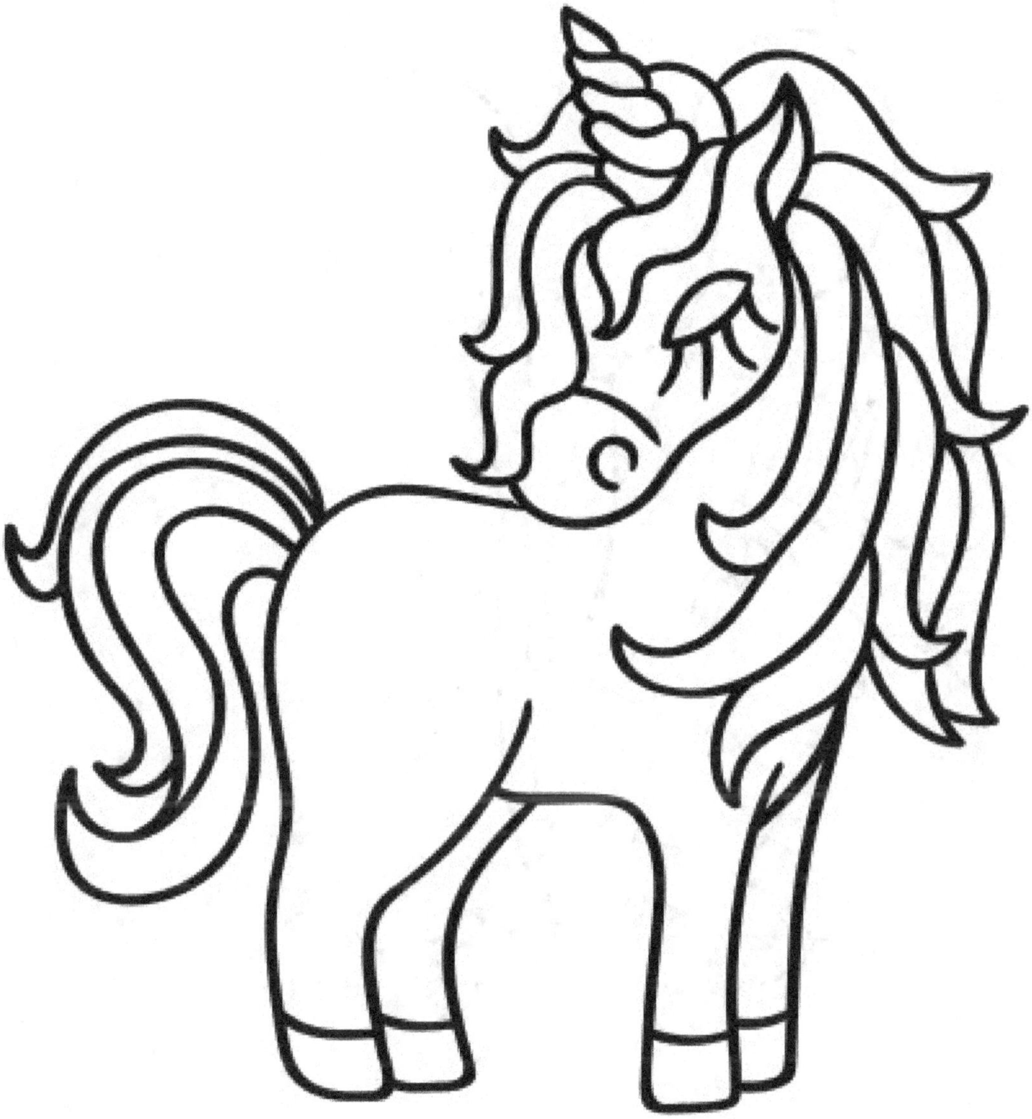

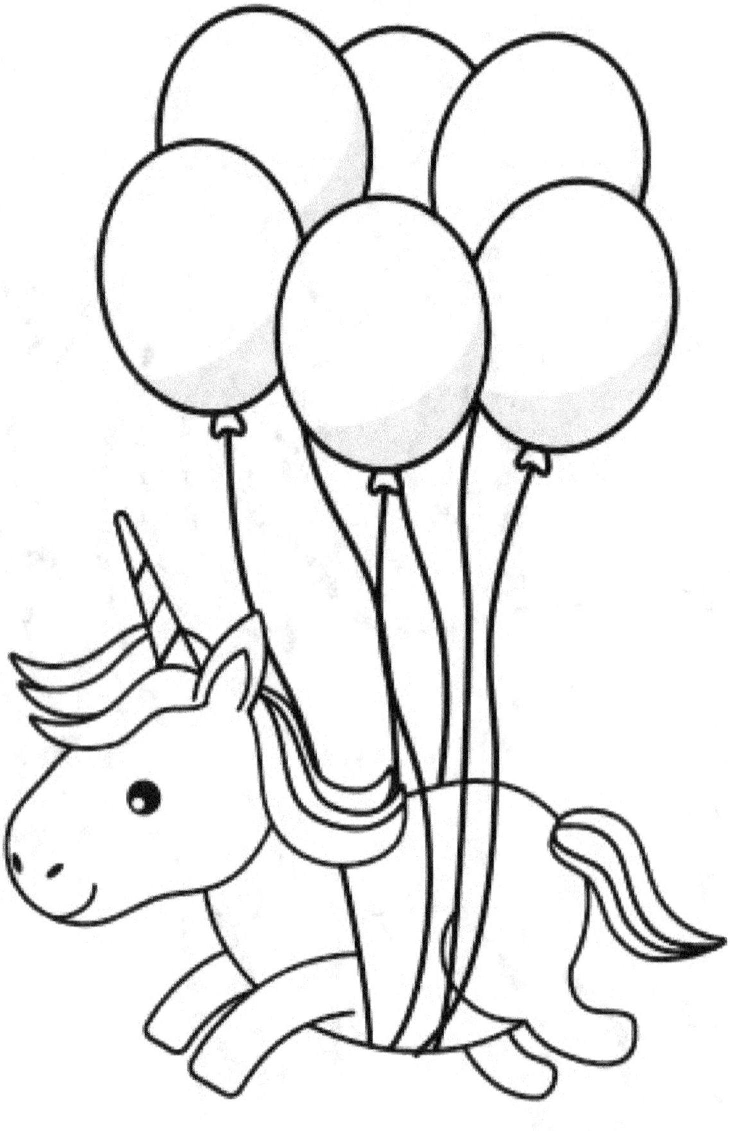

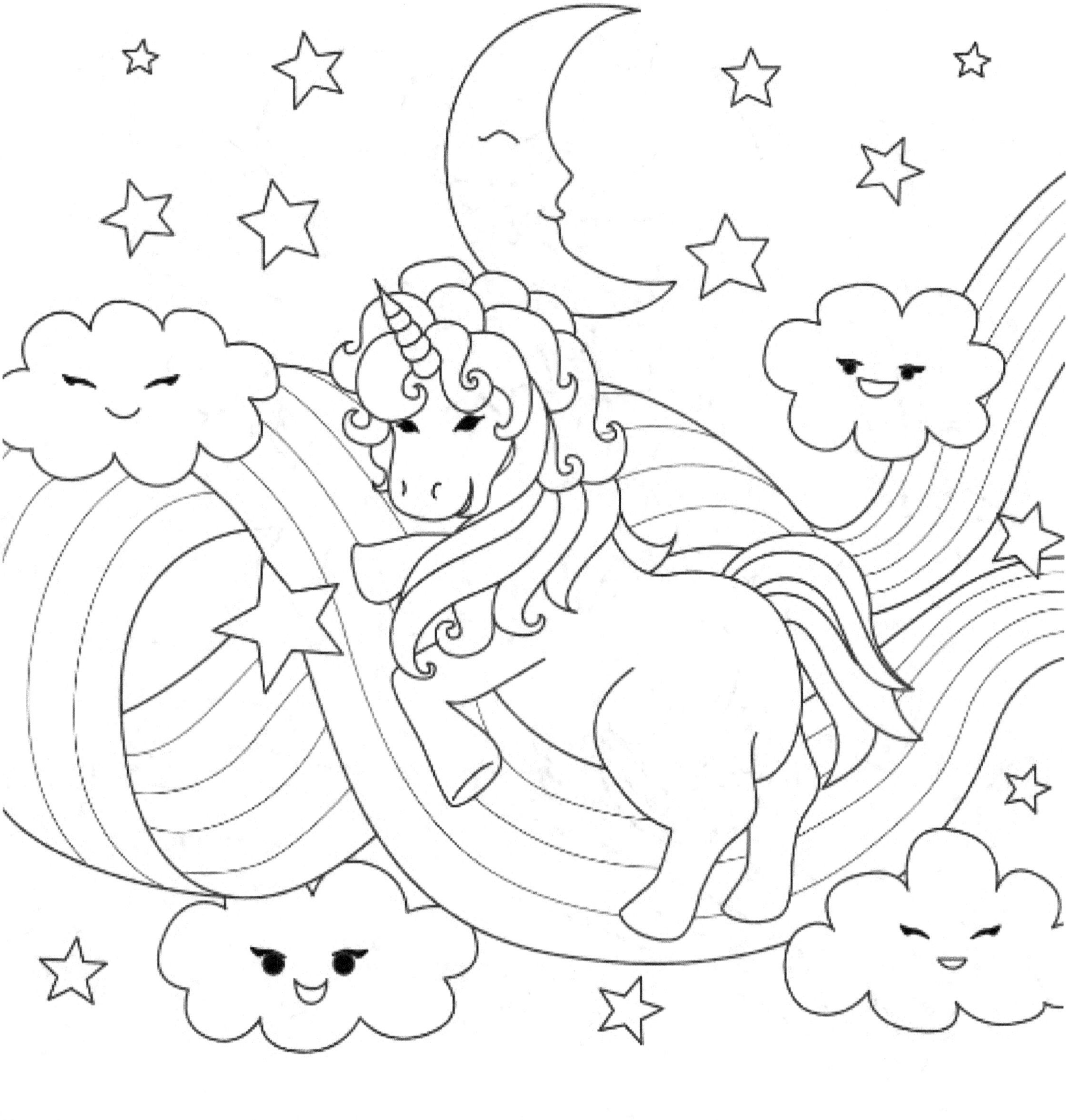

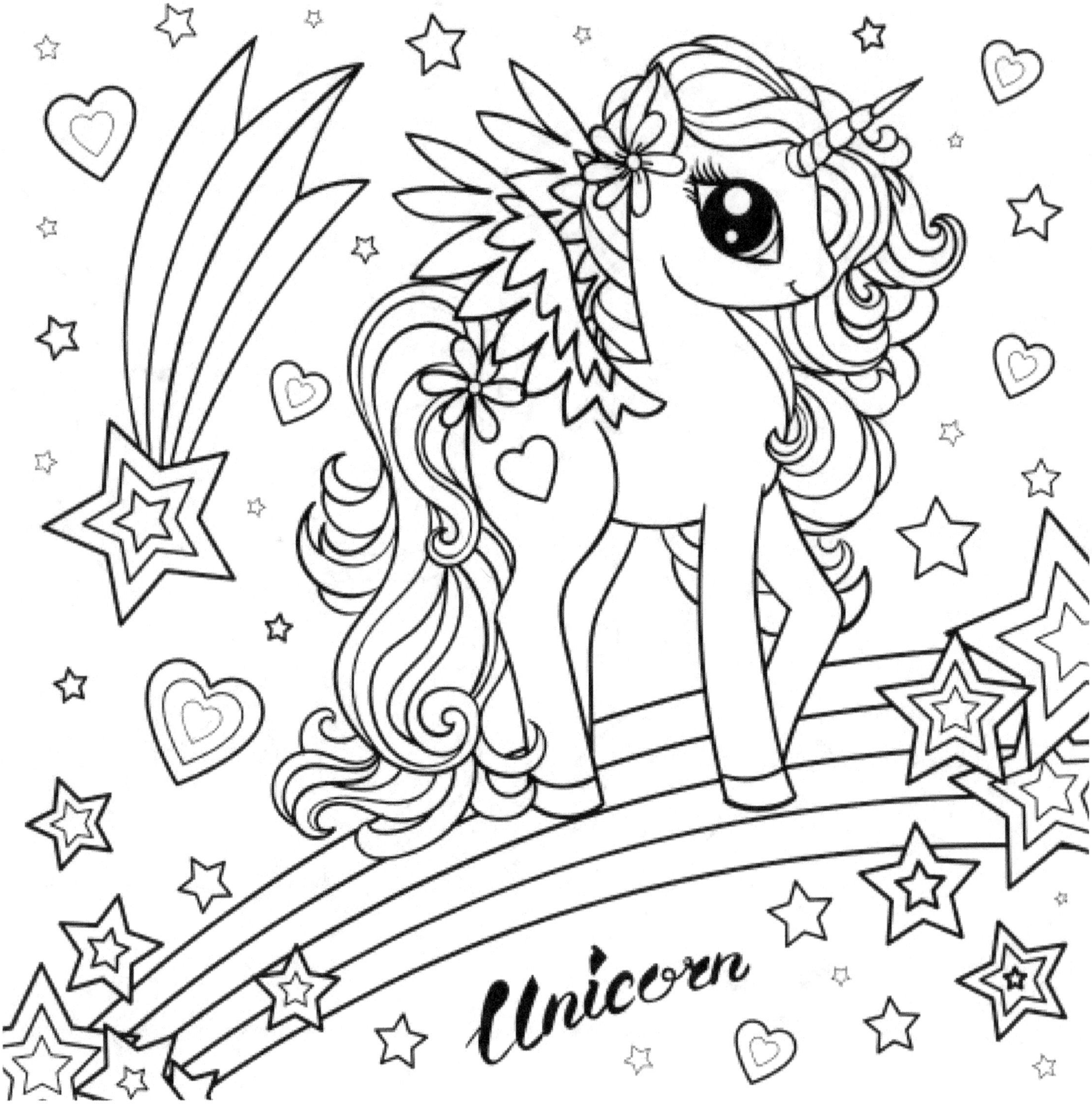
Unicorn

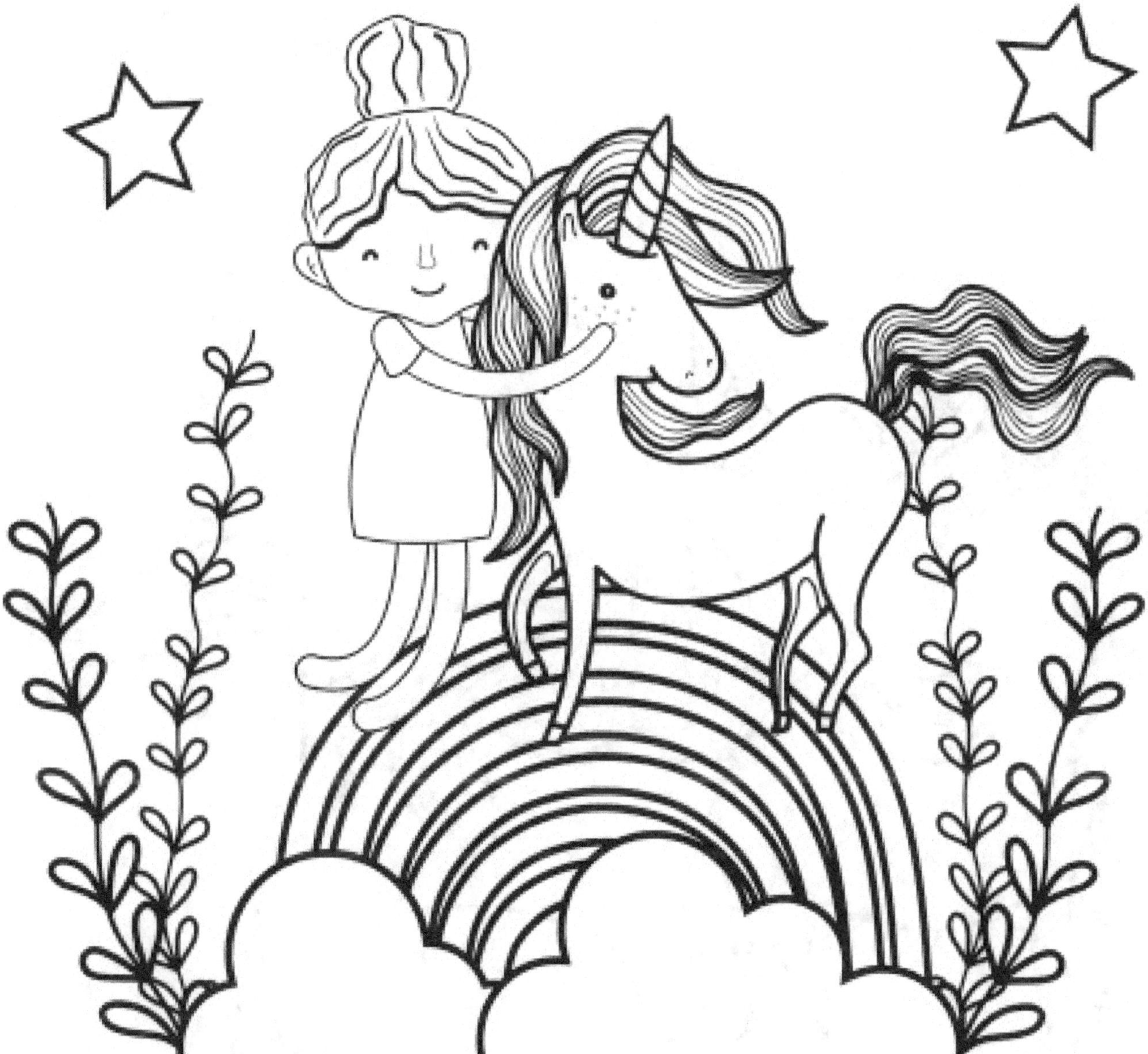

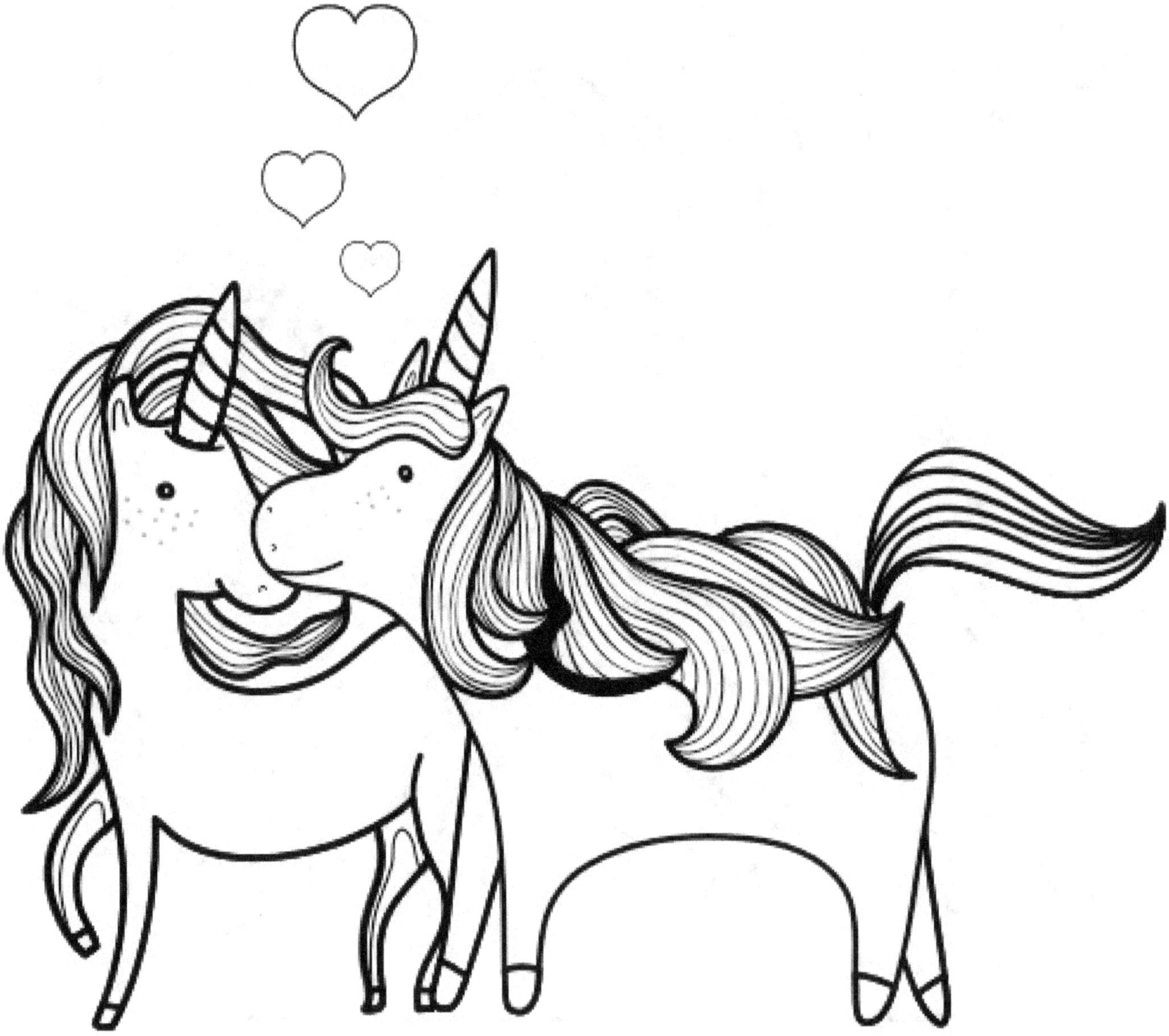

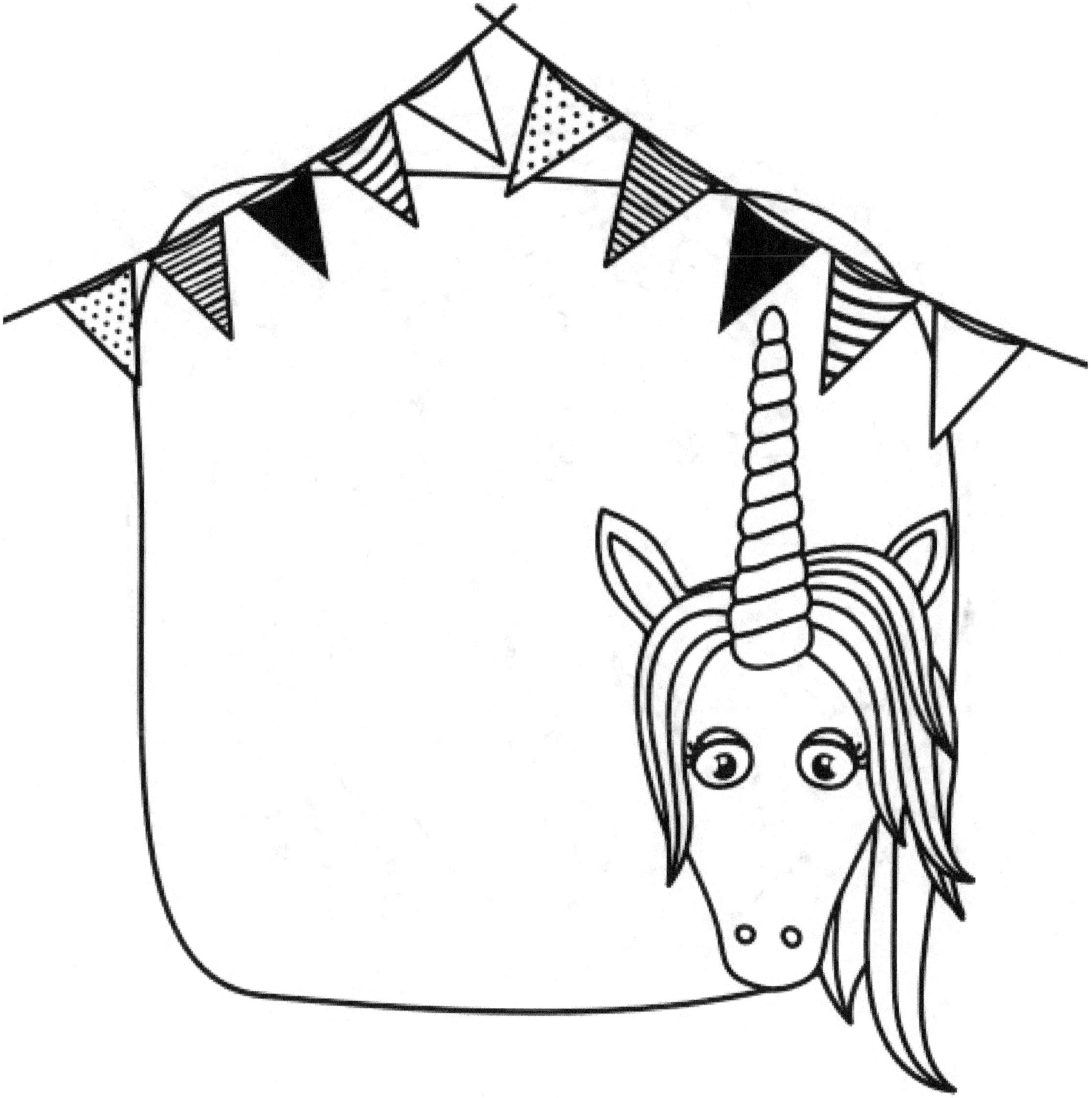

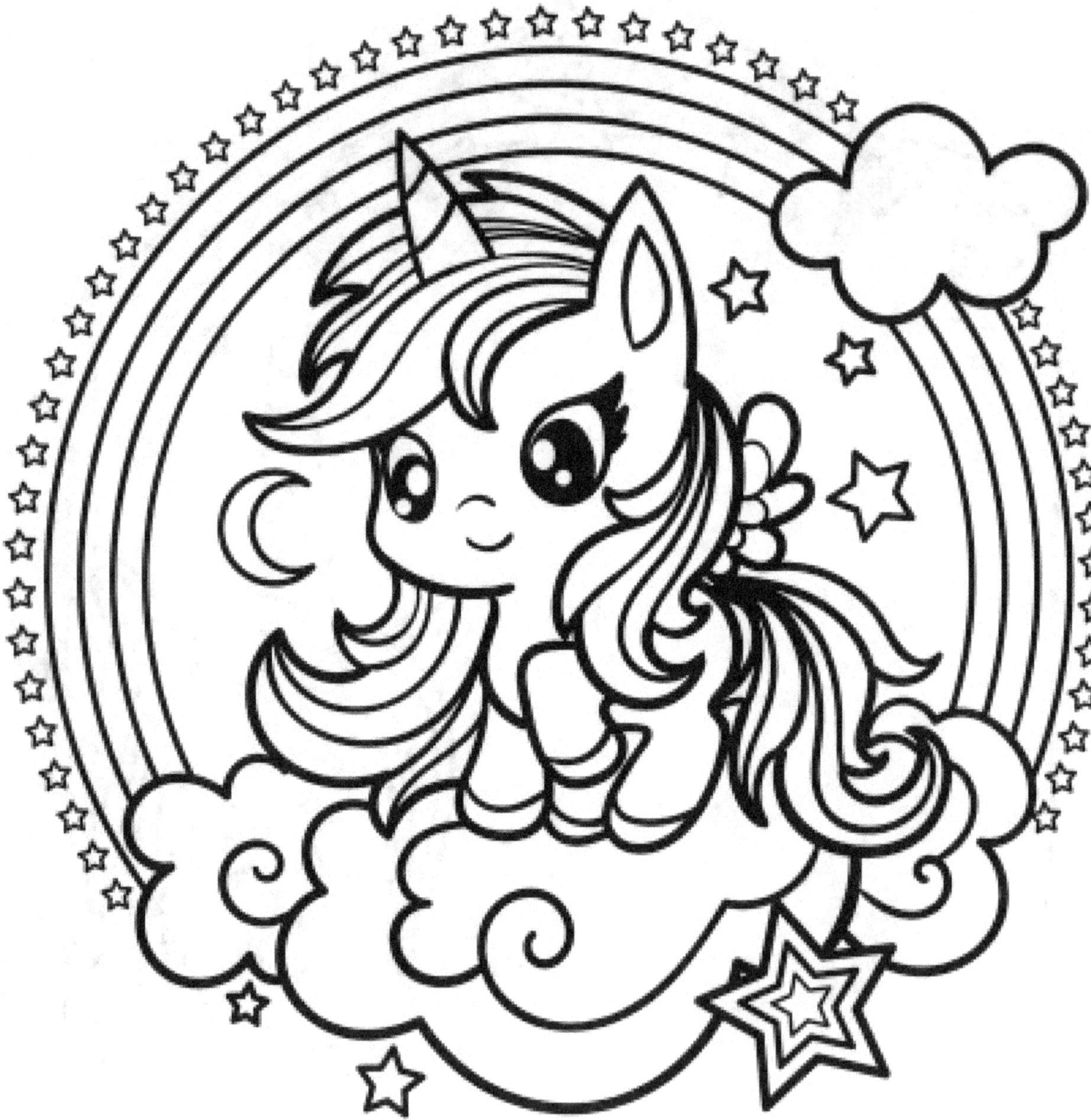

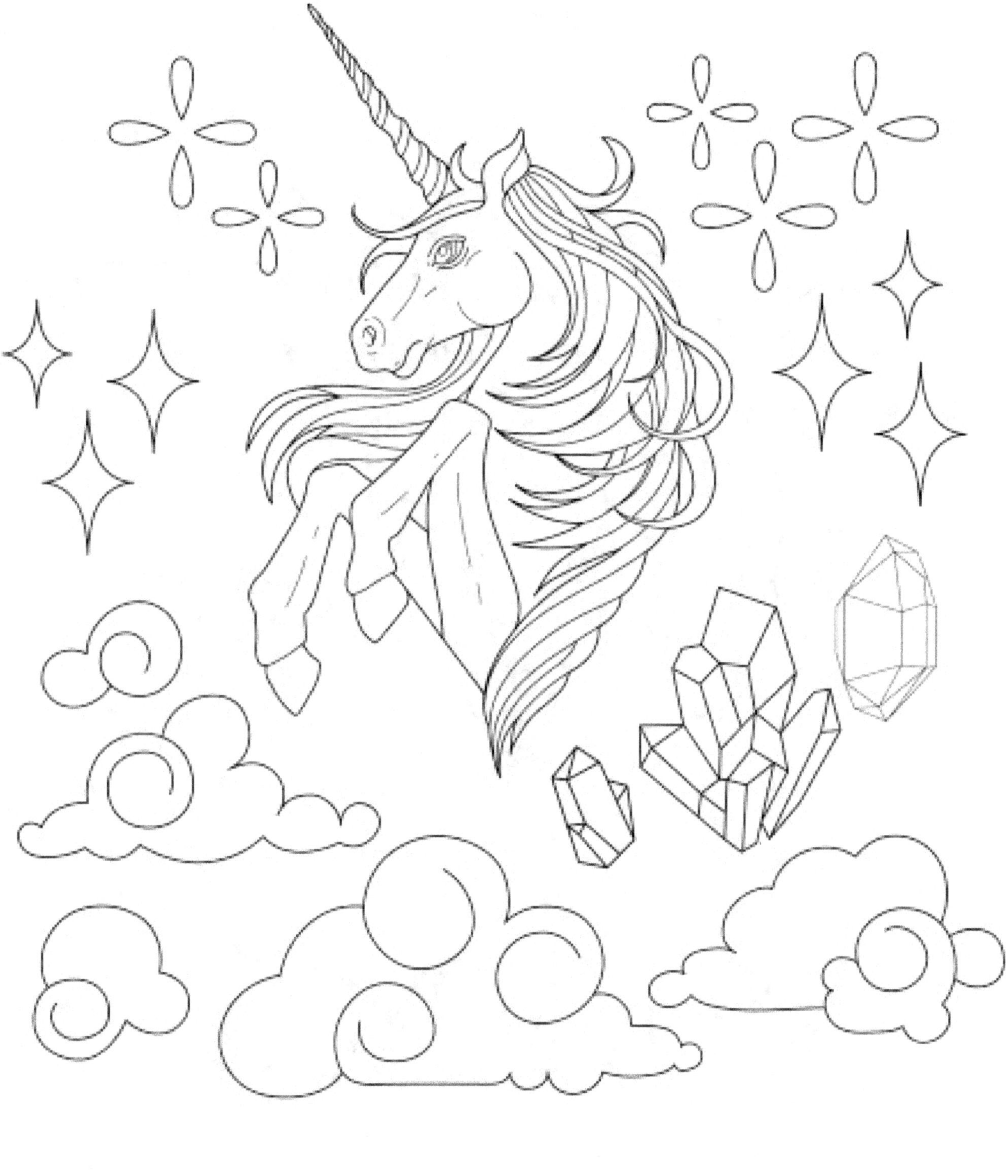

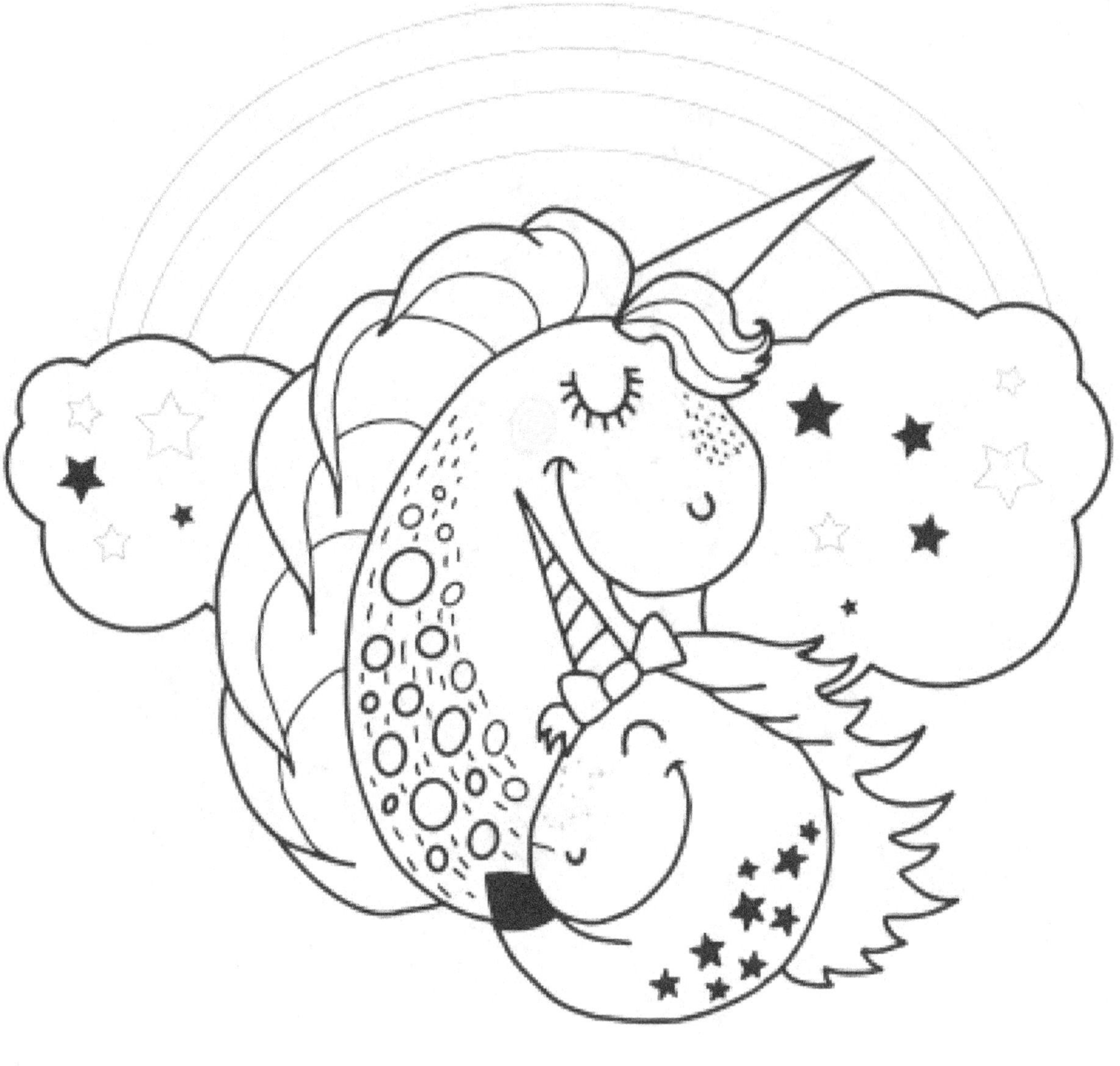

MAGIC

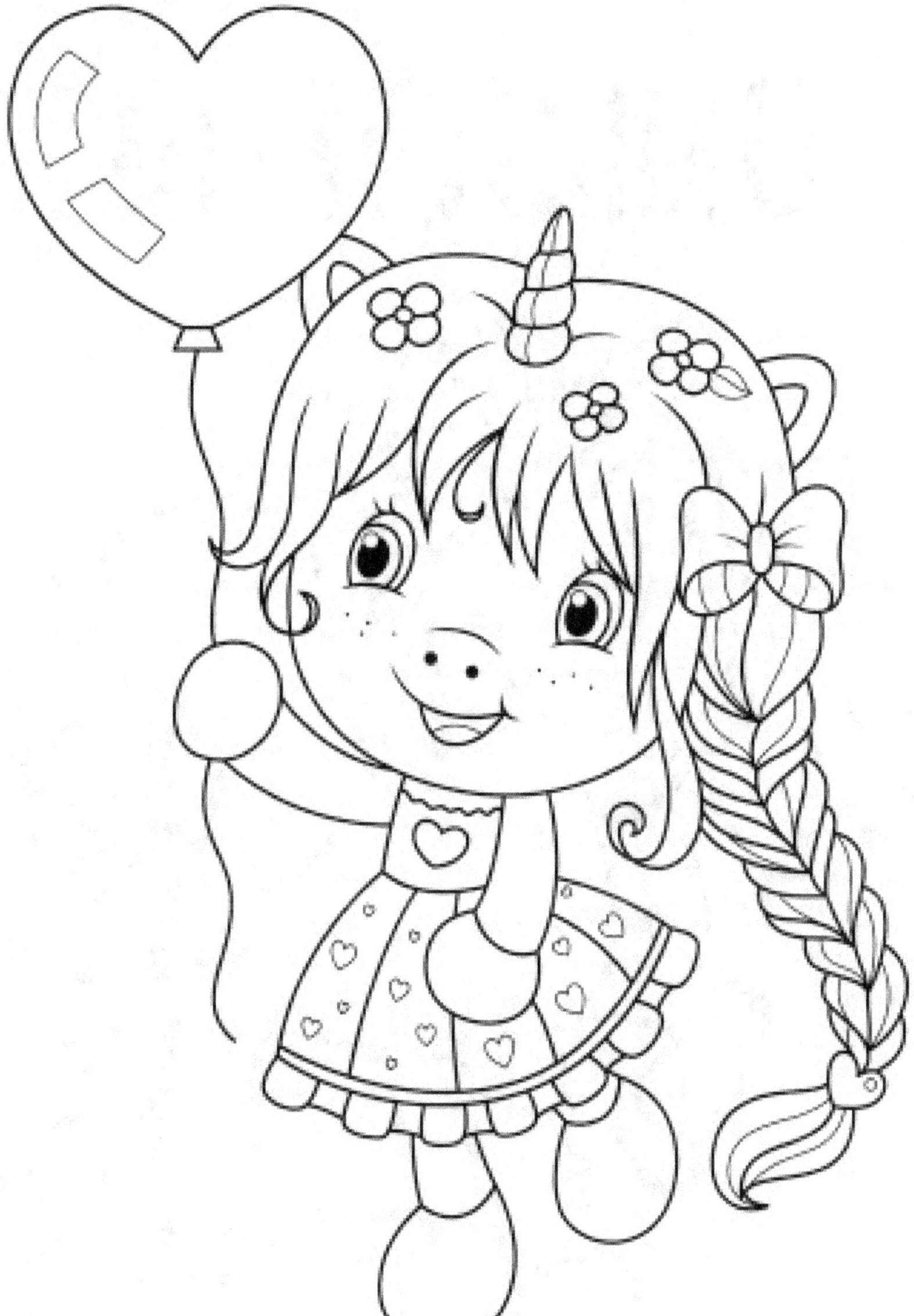

UNICORN

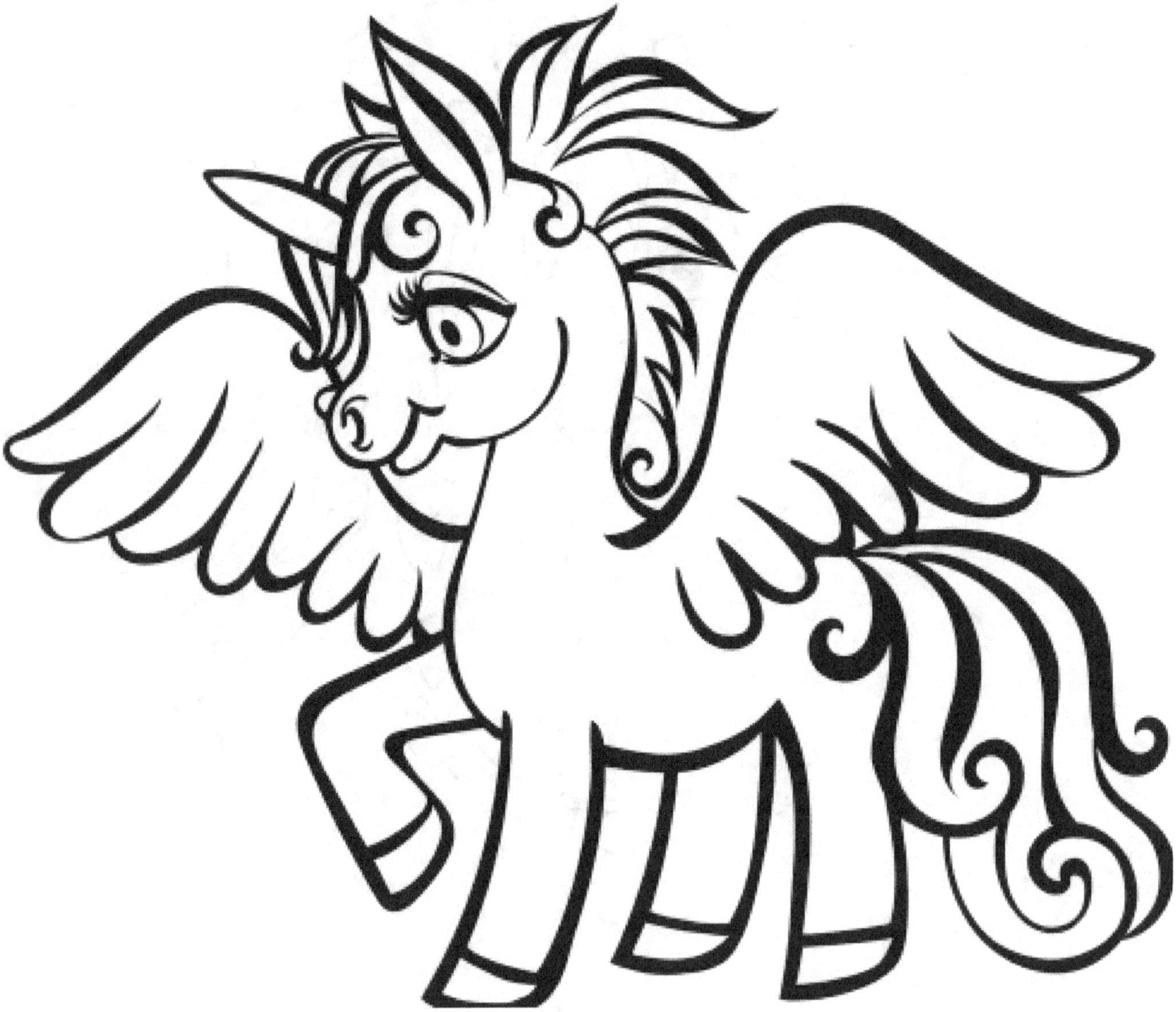

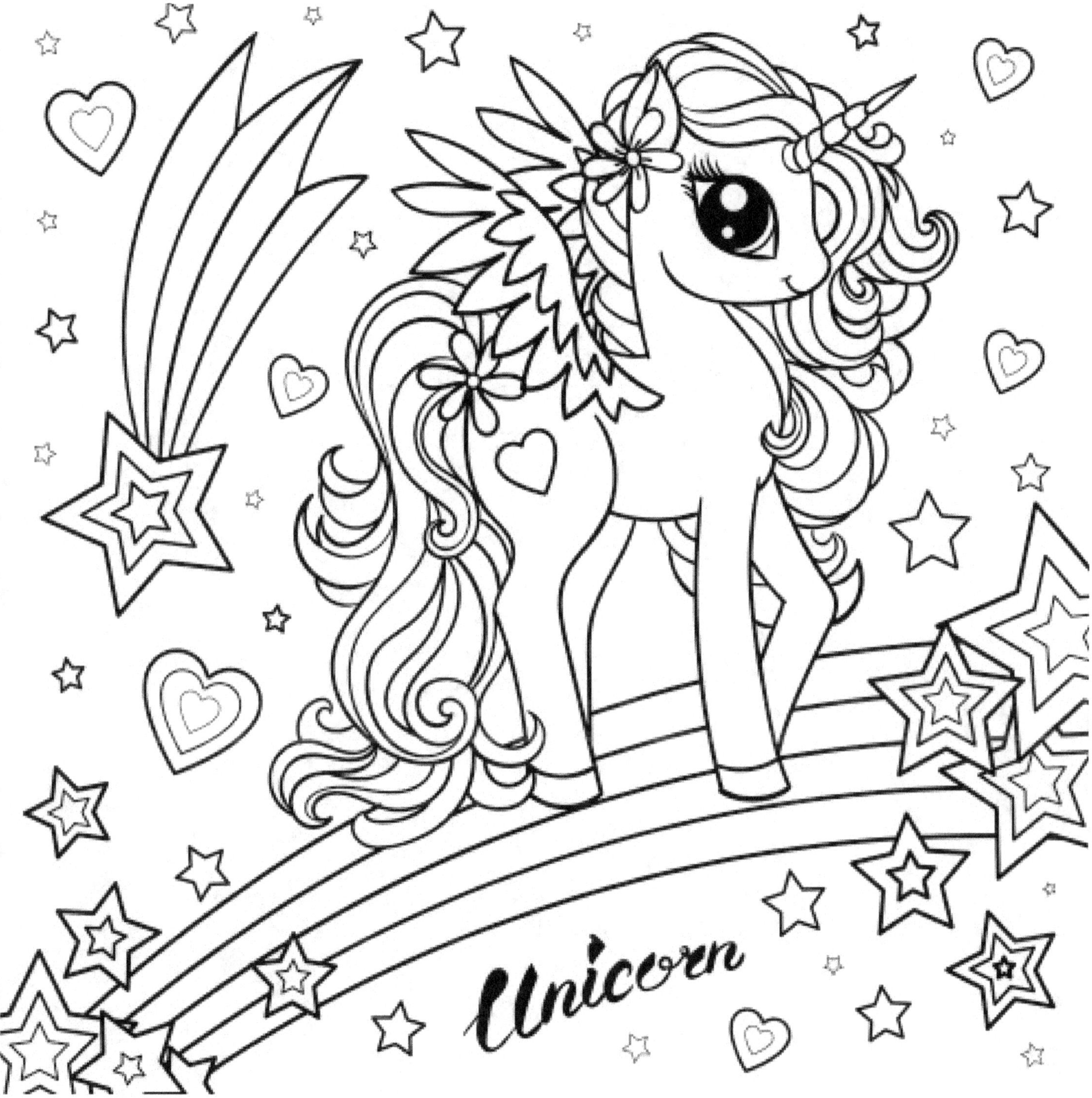
Unicorn

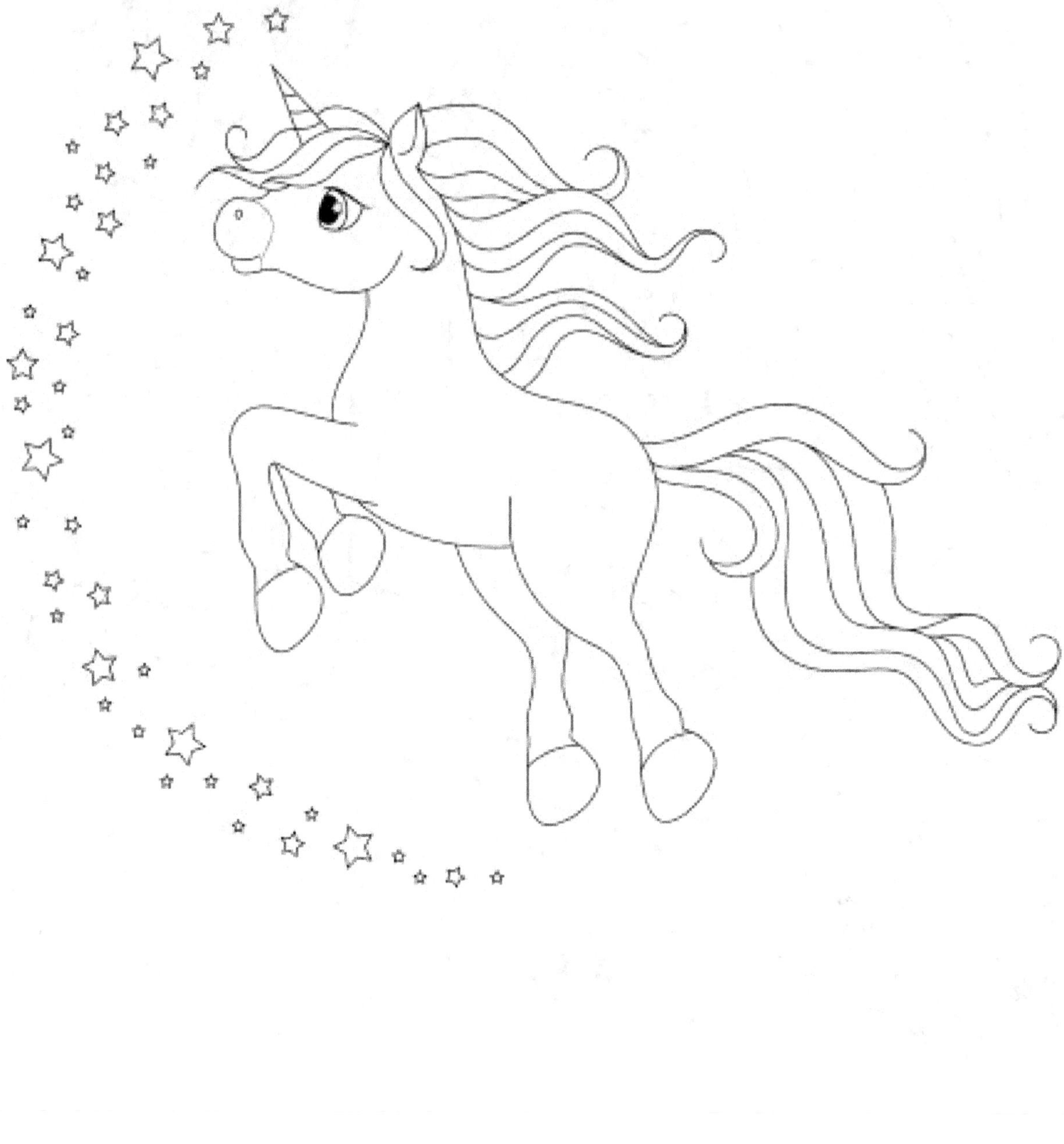

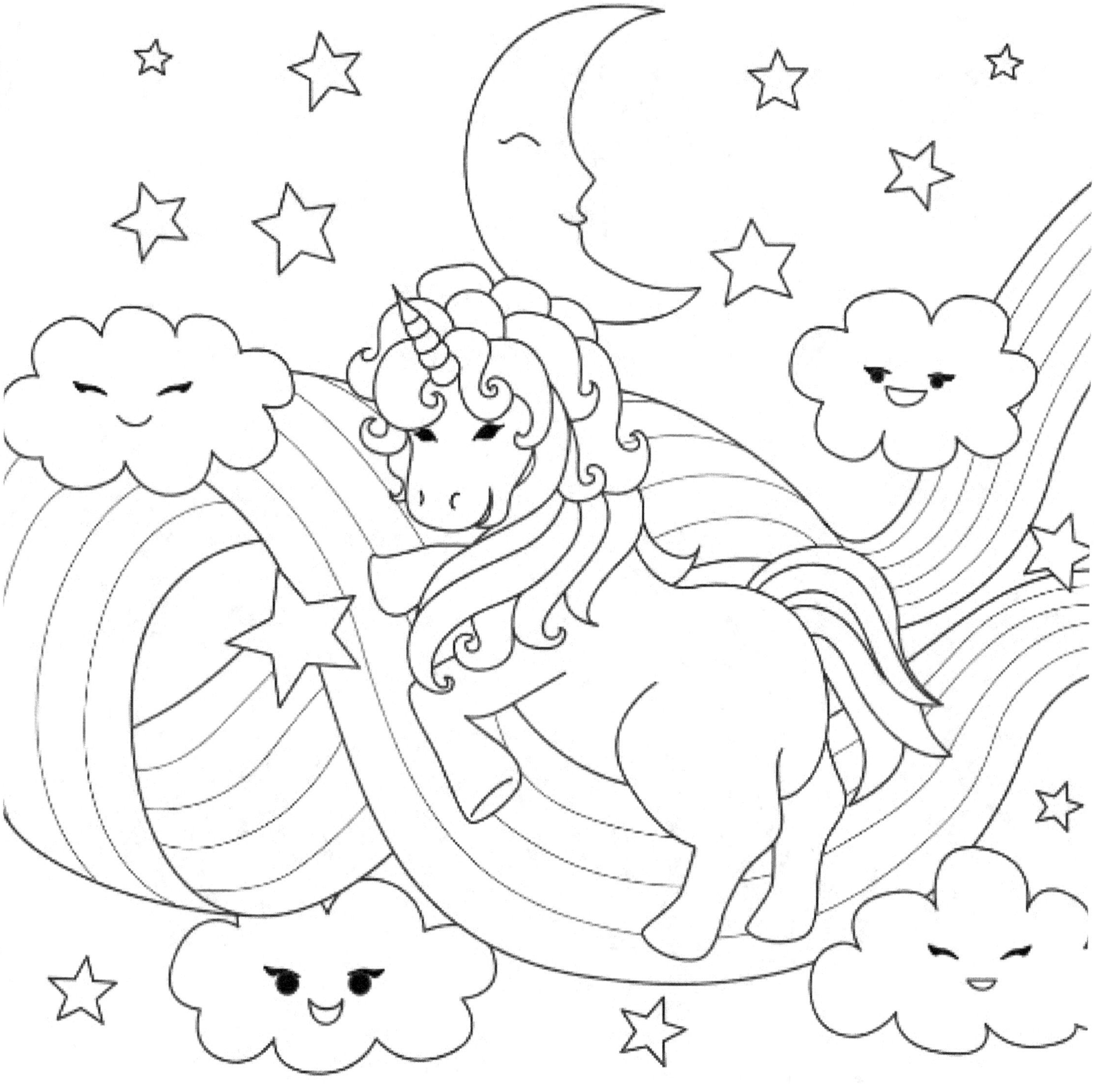

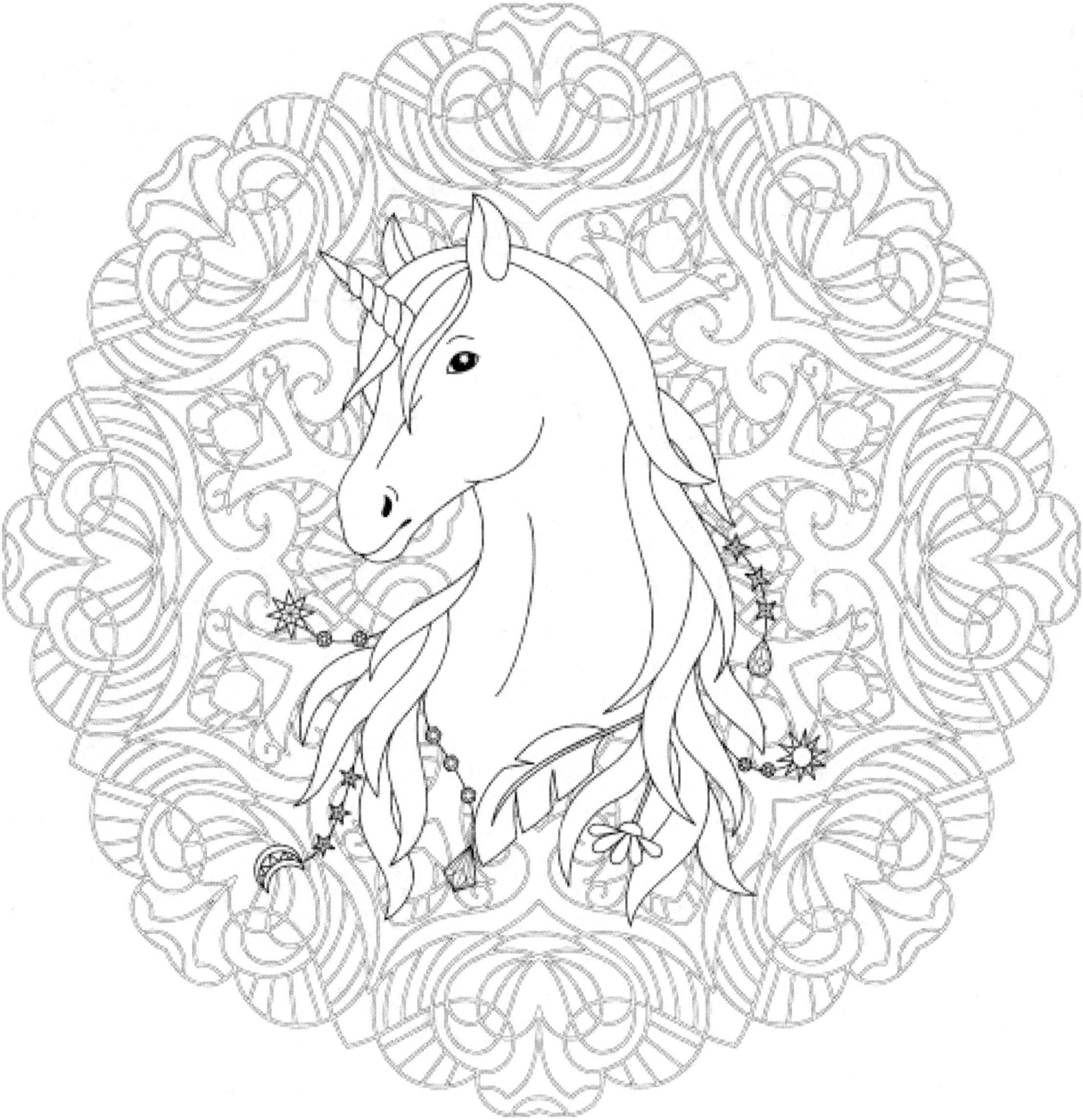

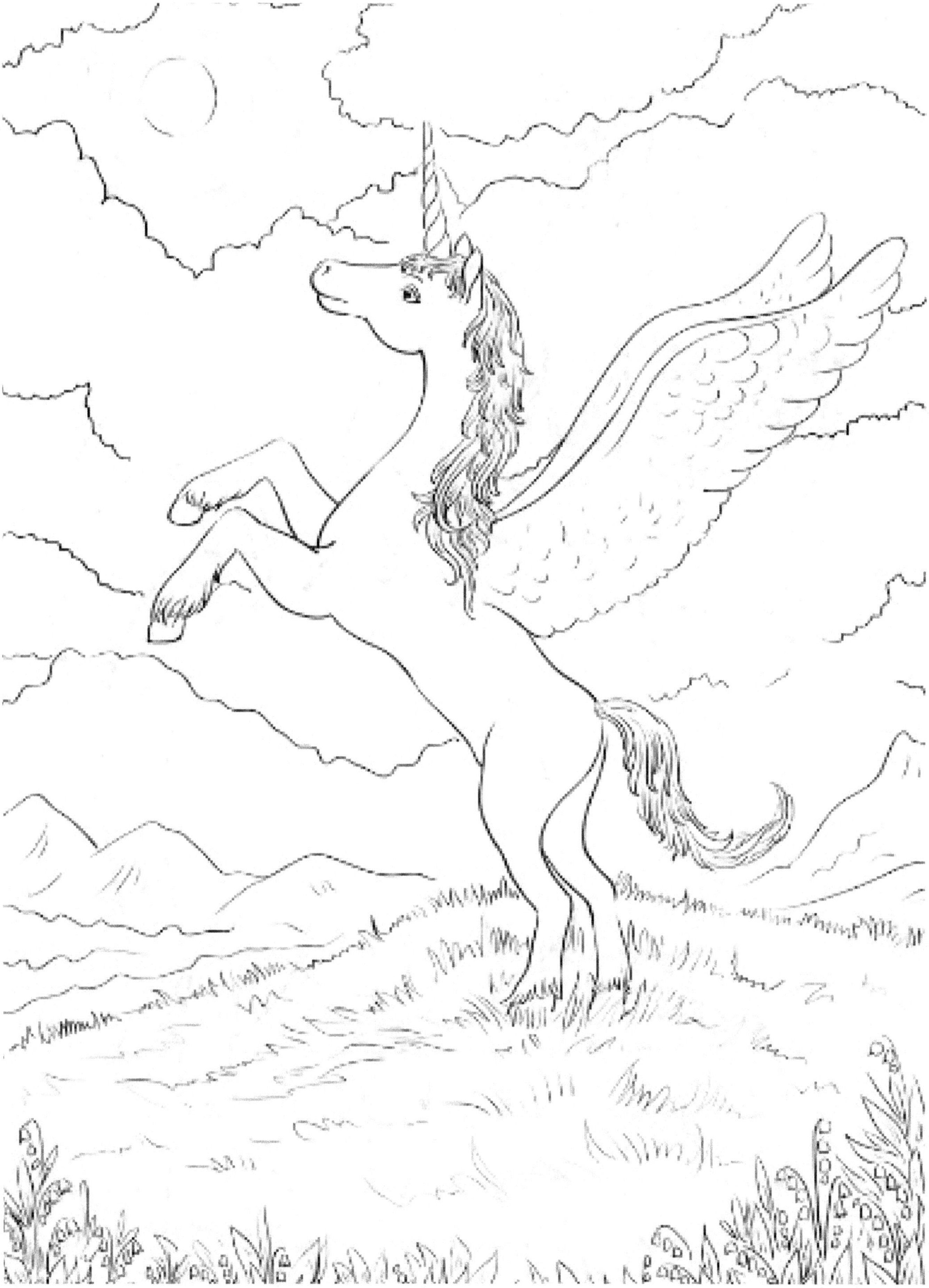

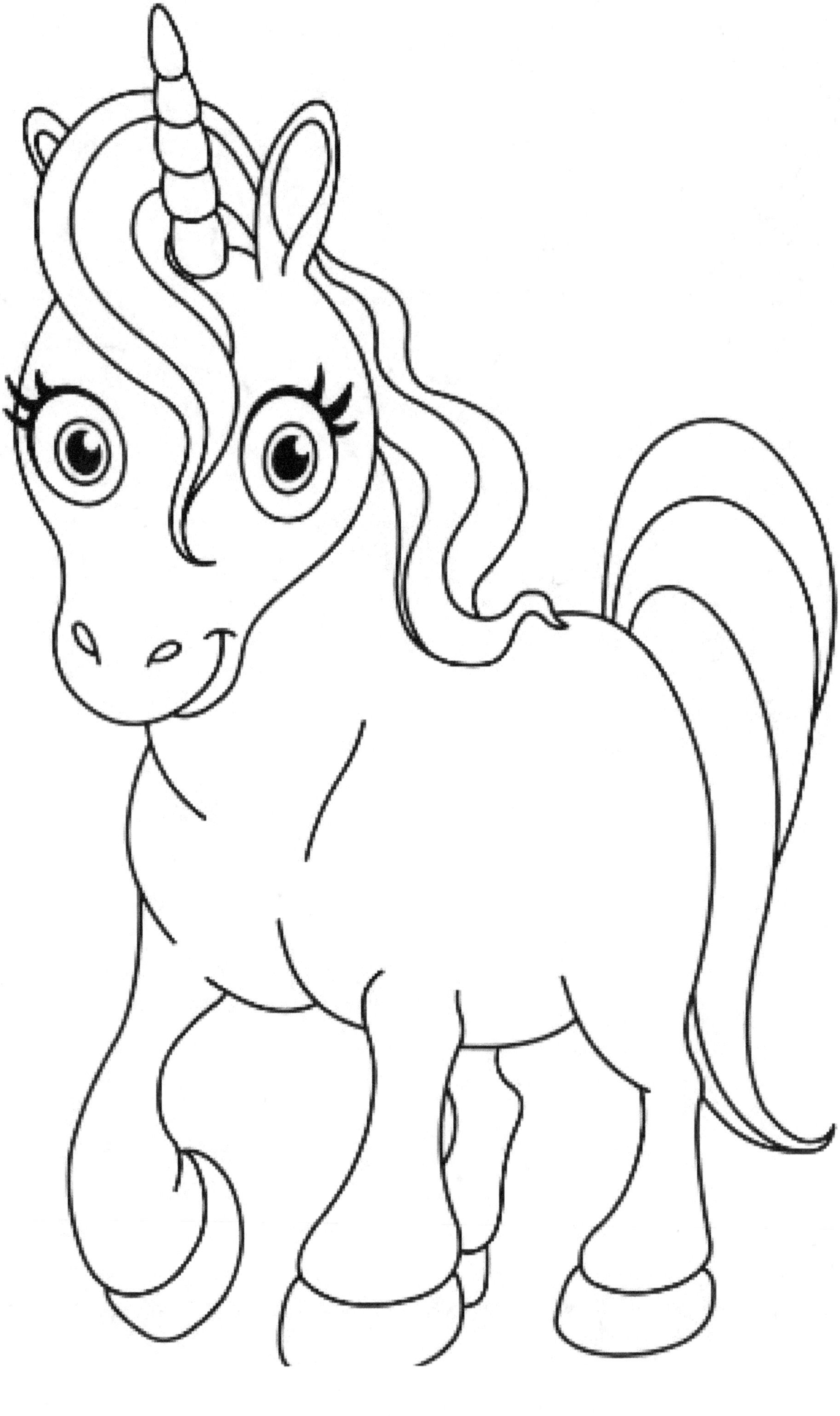

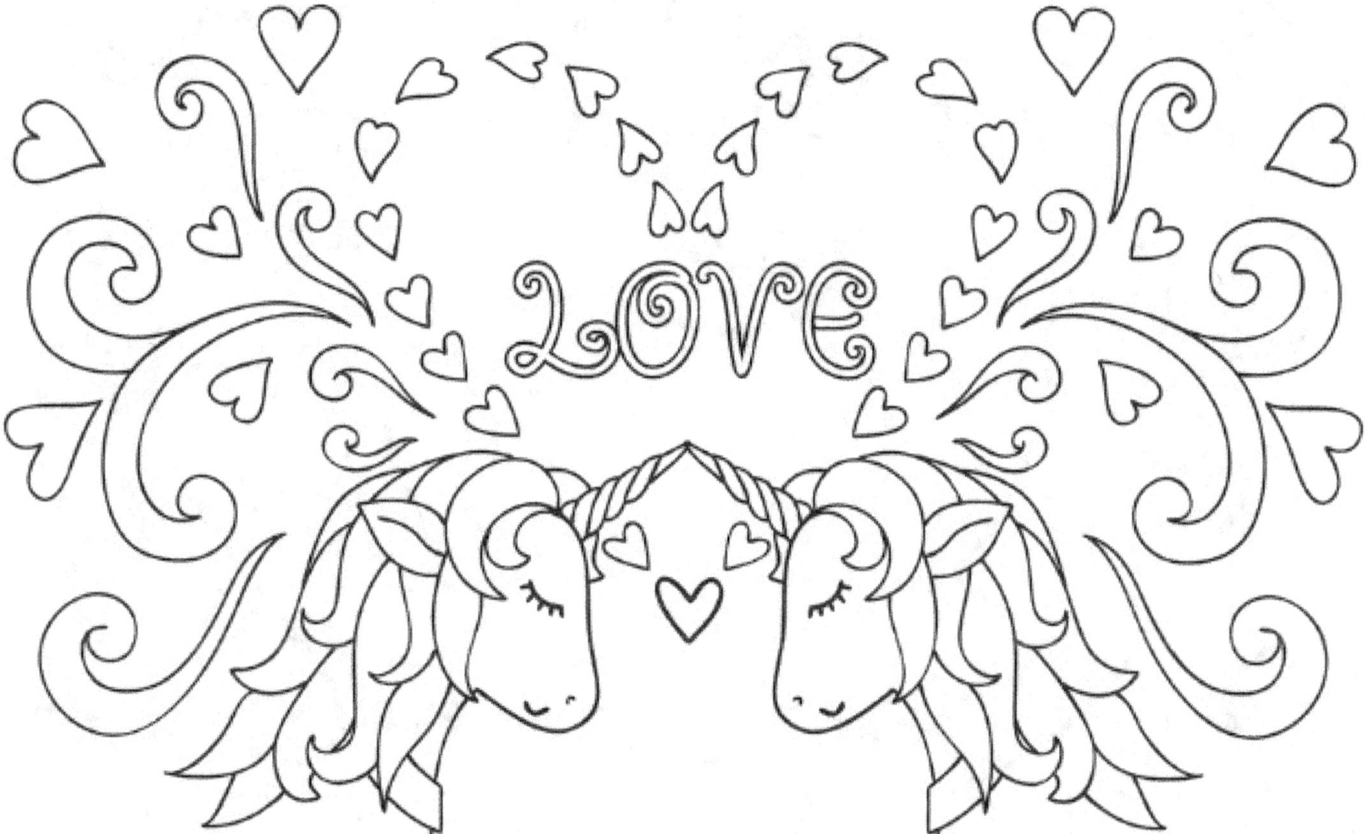
LOVE

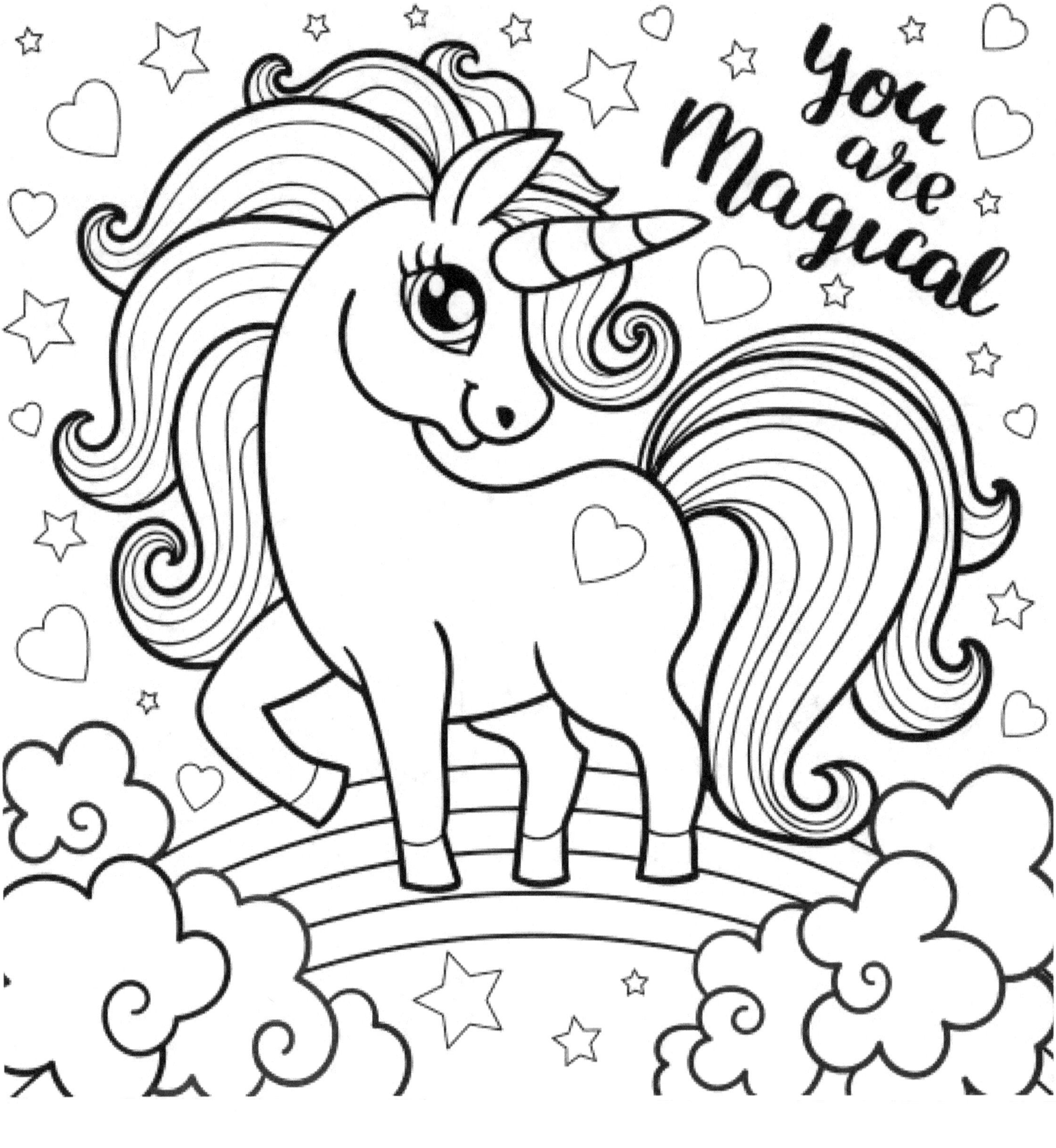
You are Magical

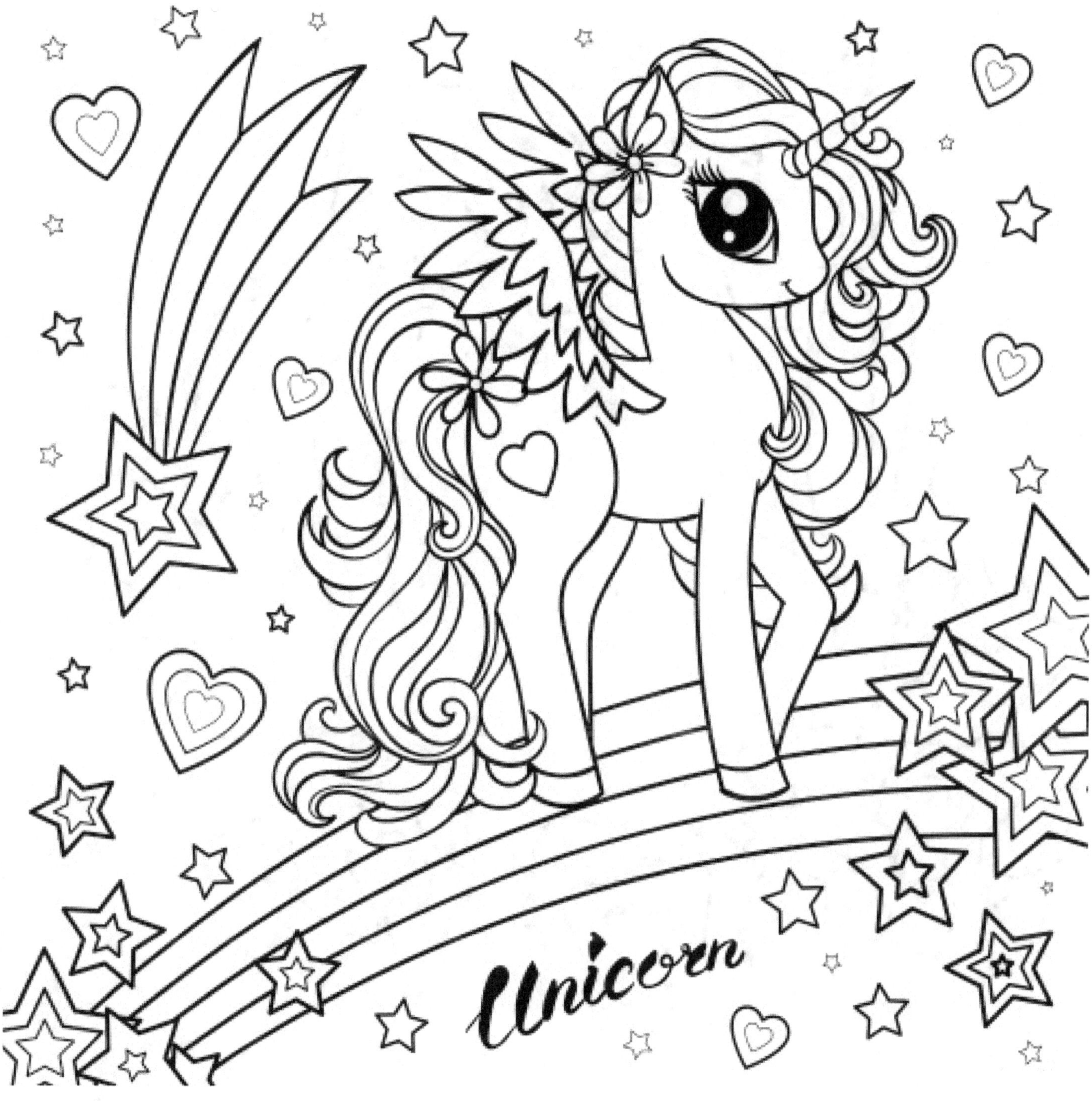
Unicorn

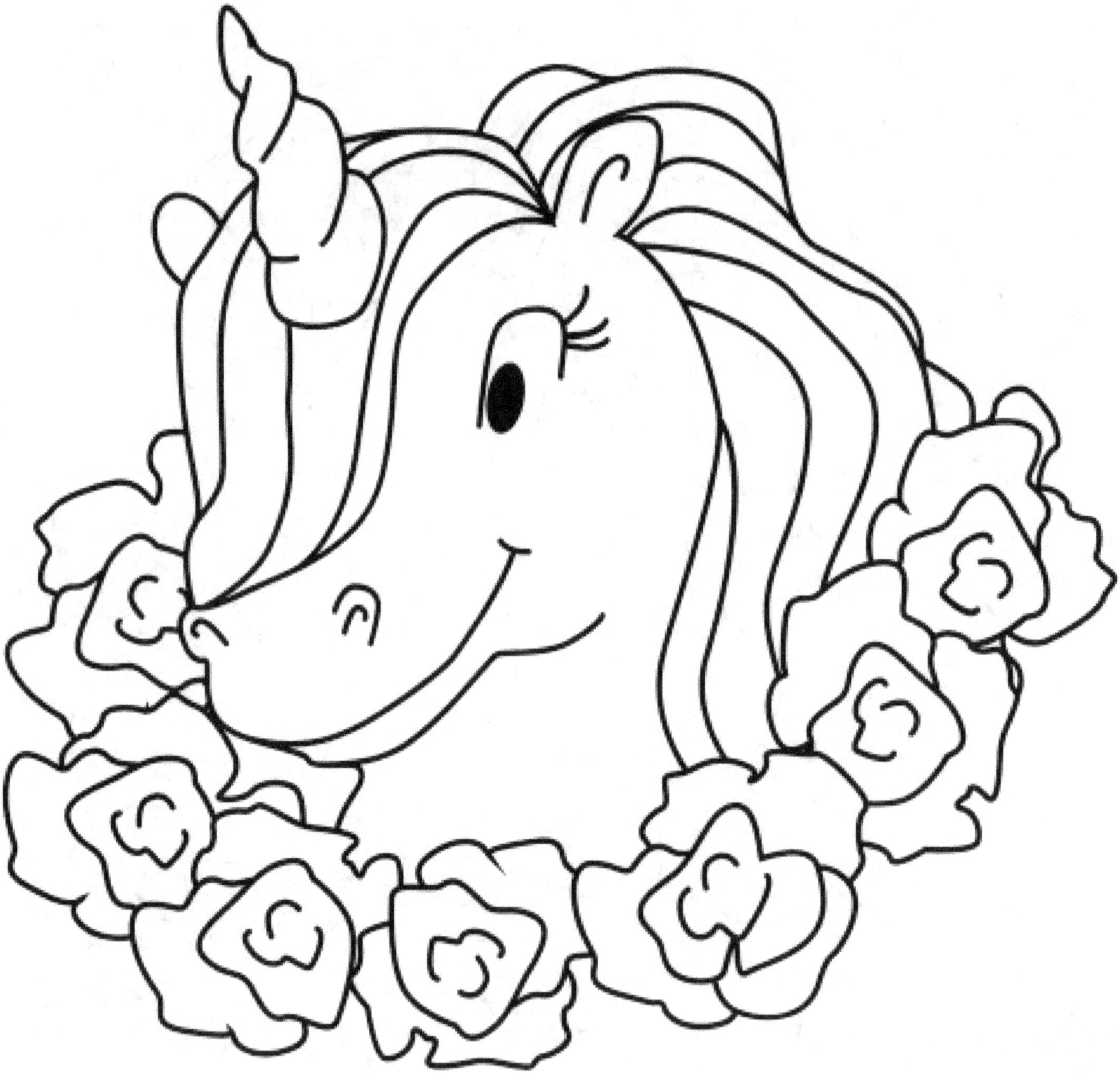

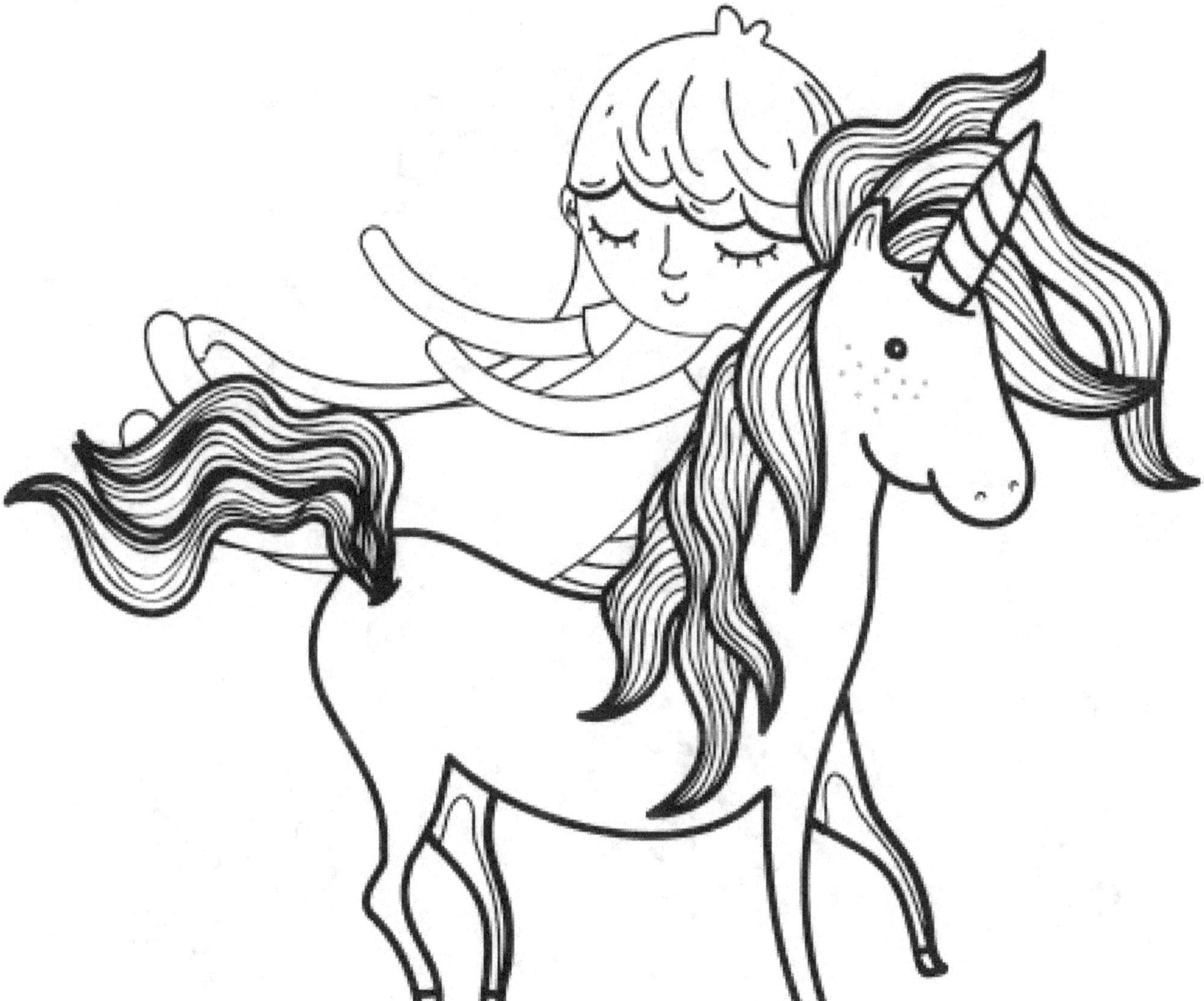

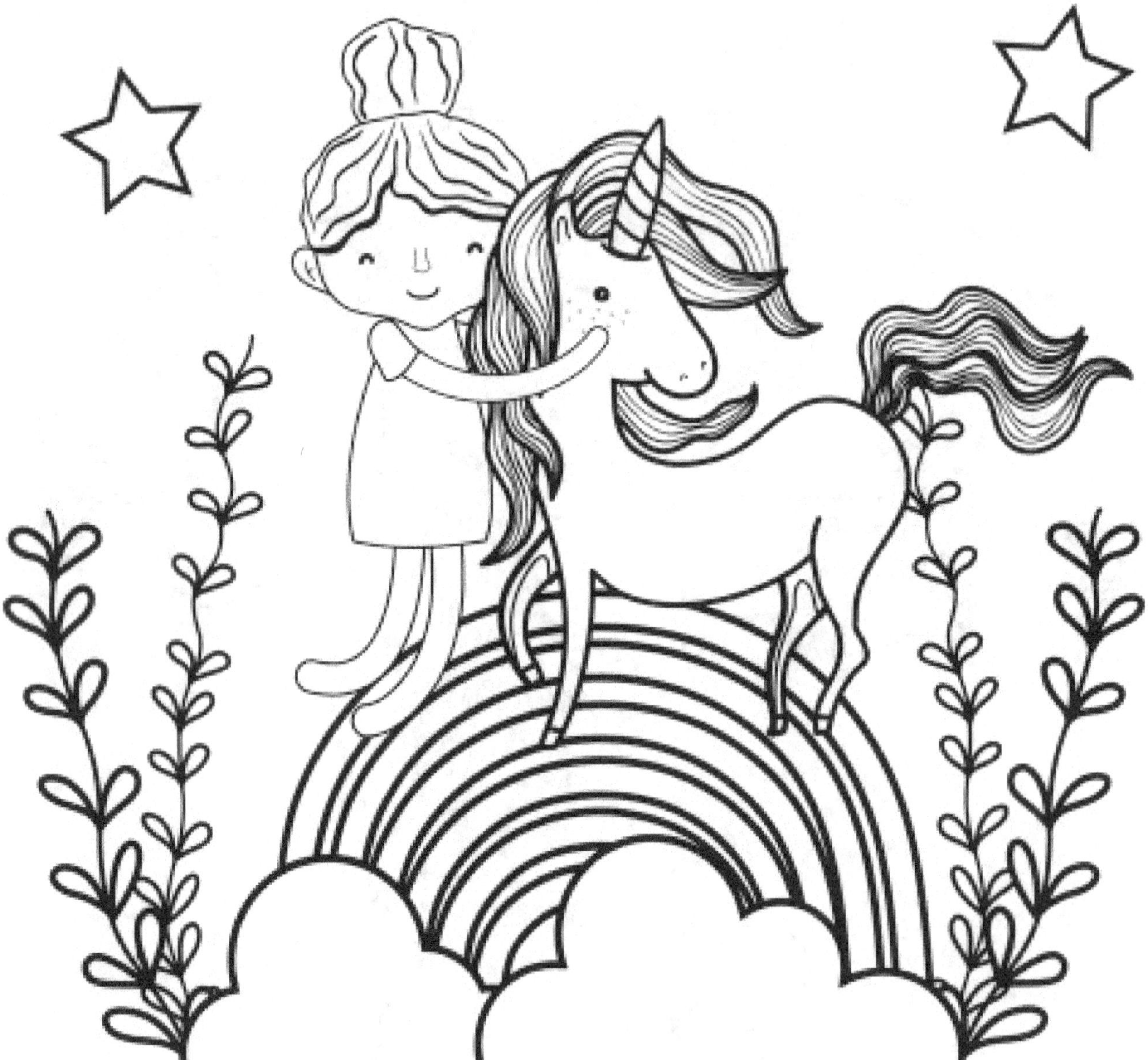

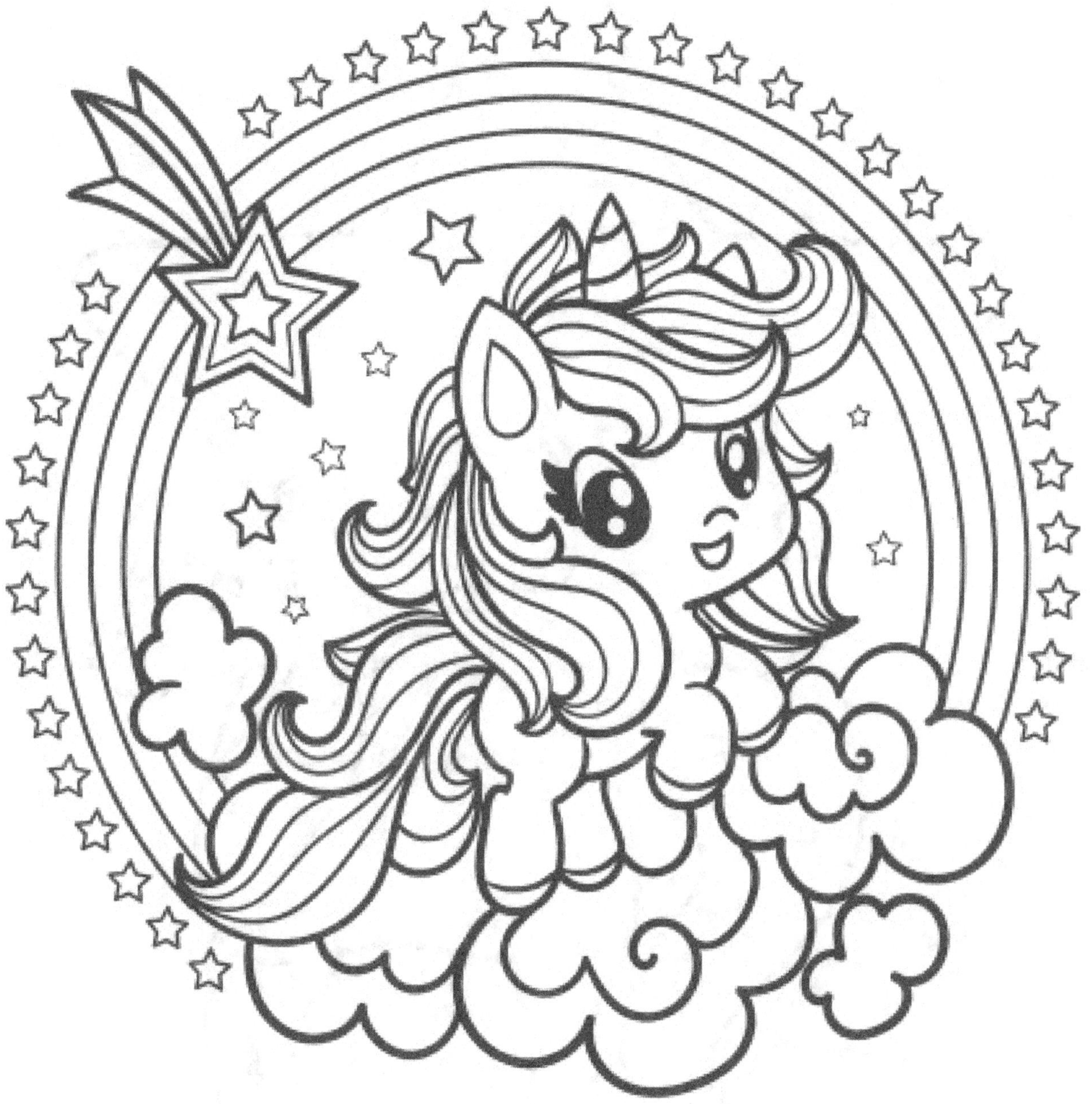

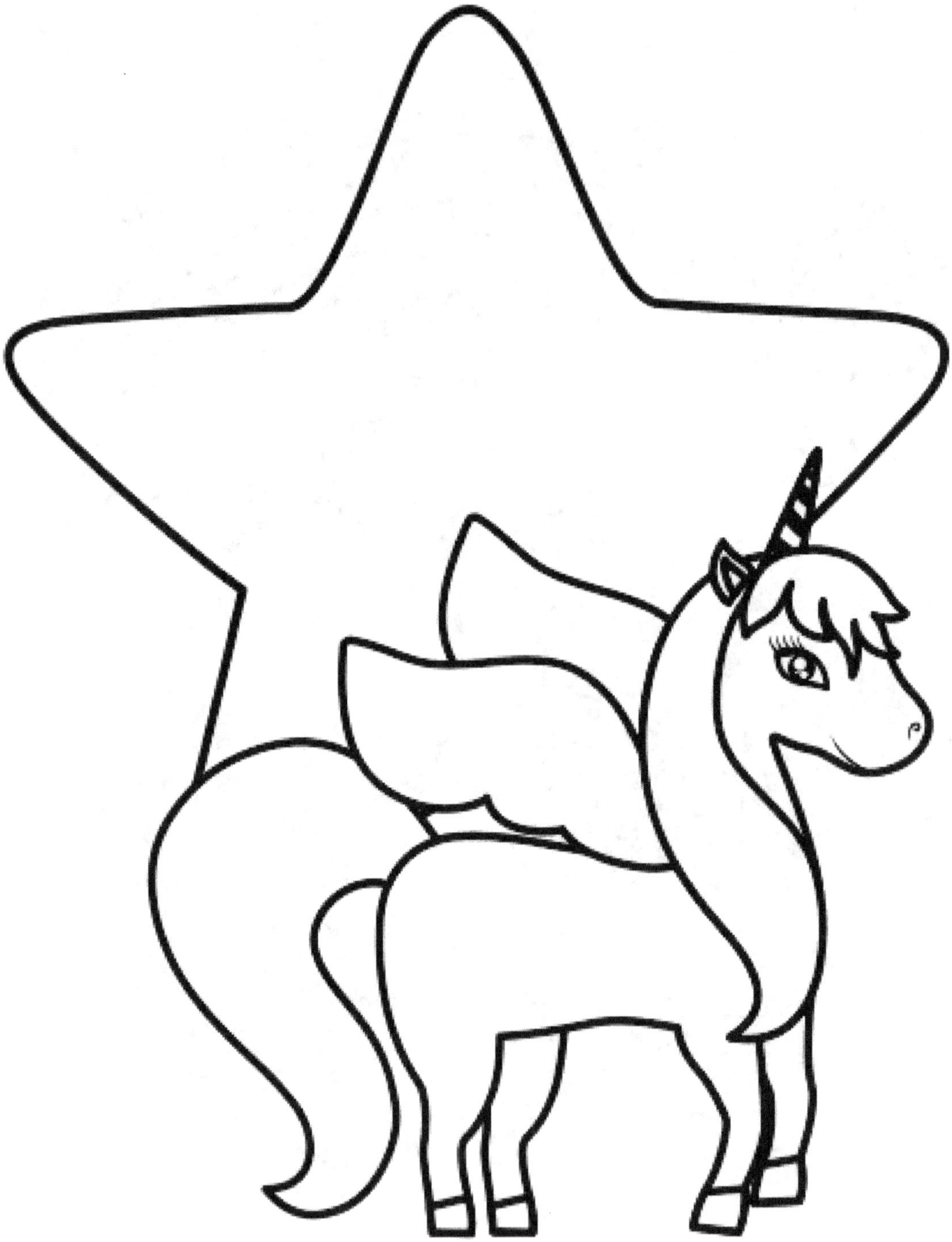

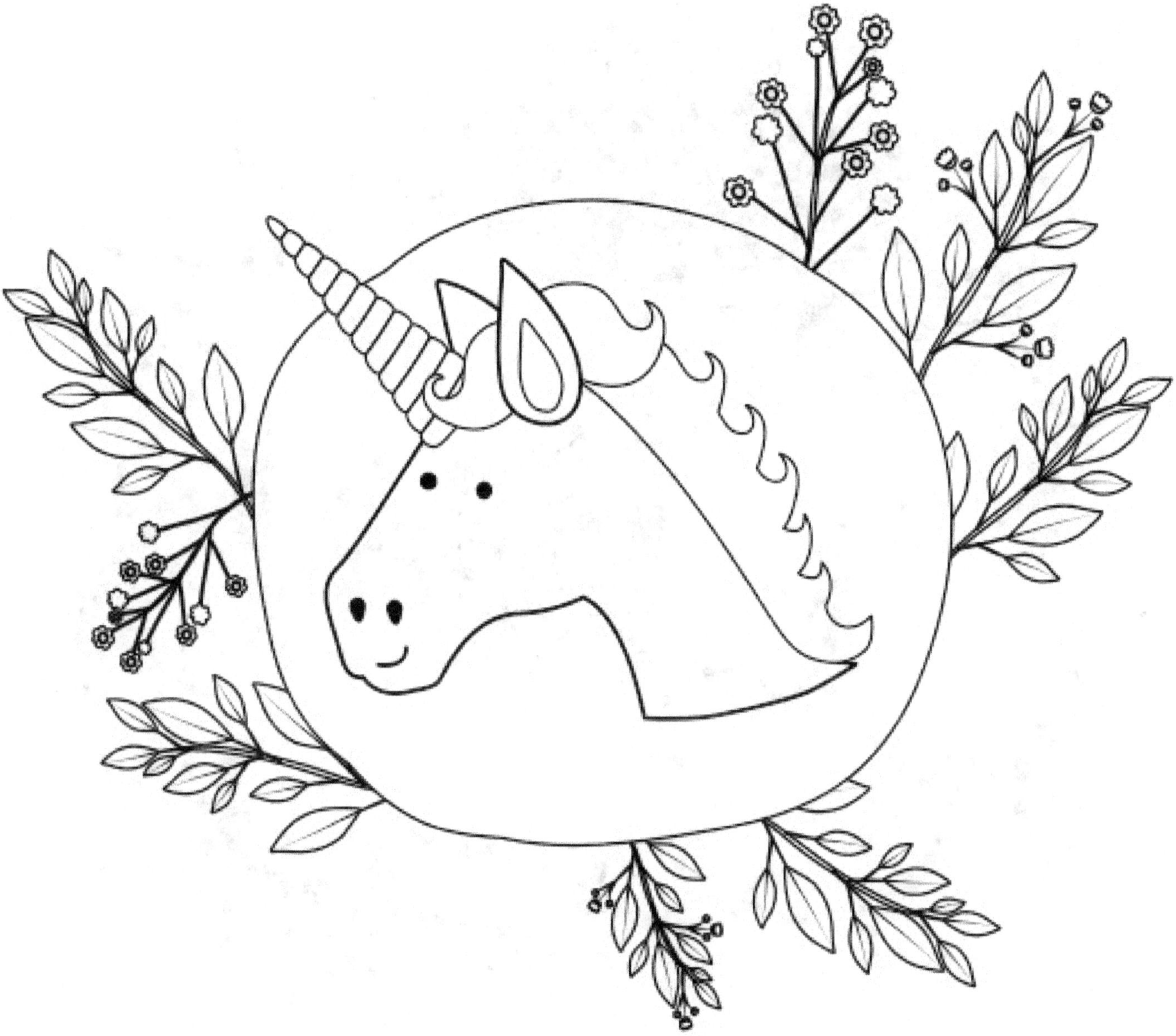

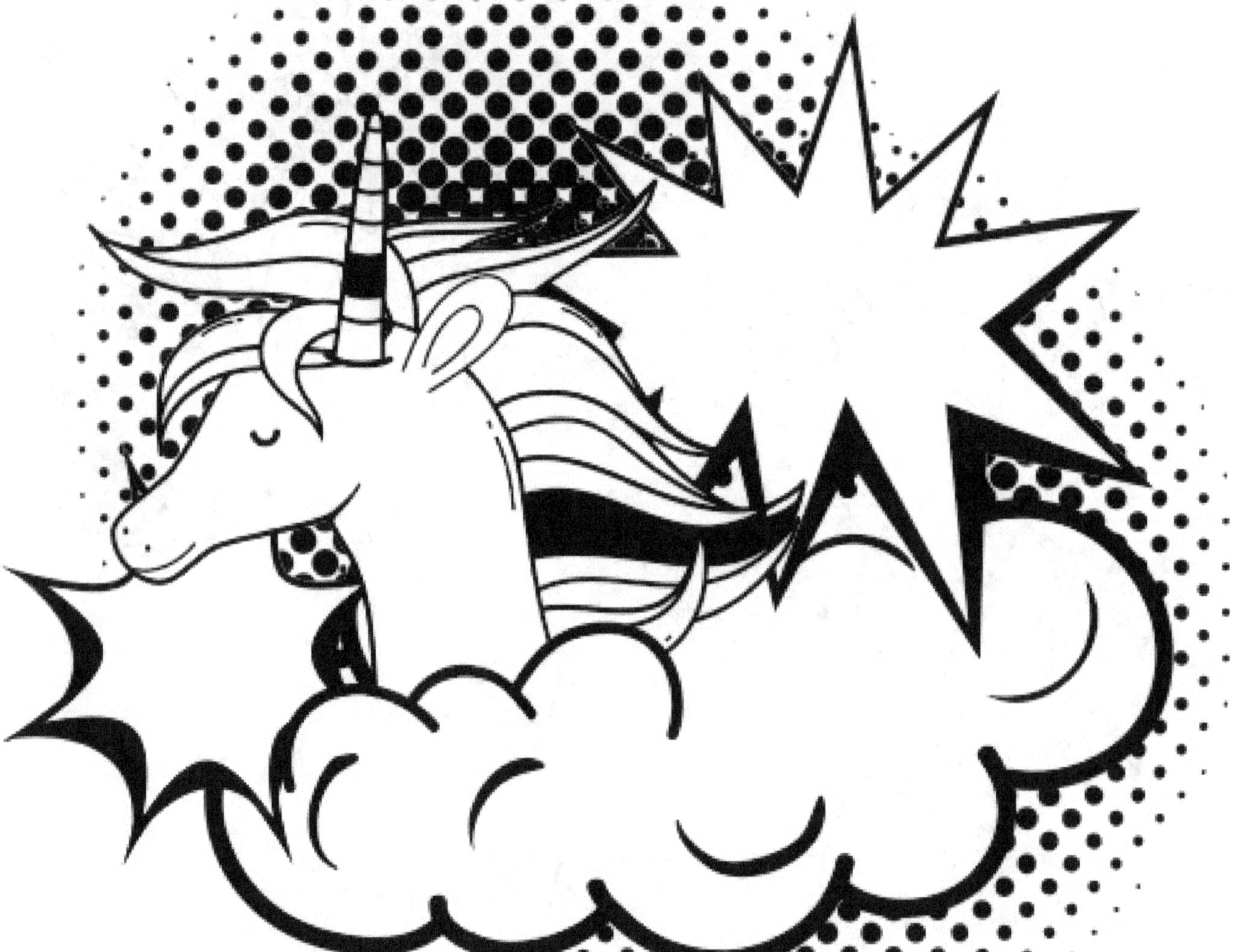

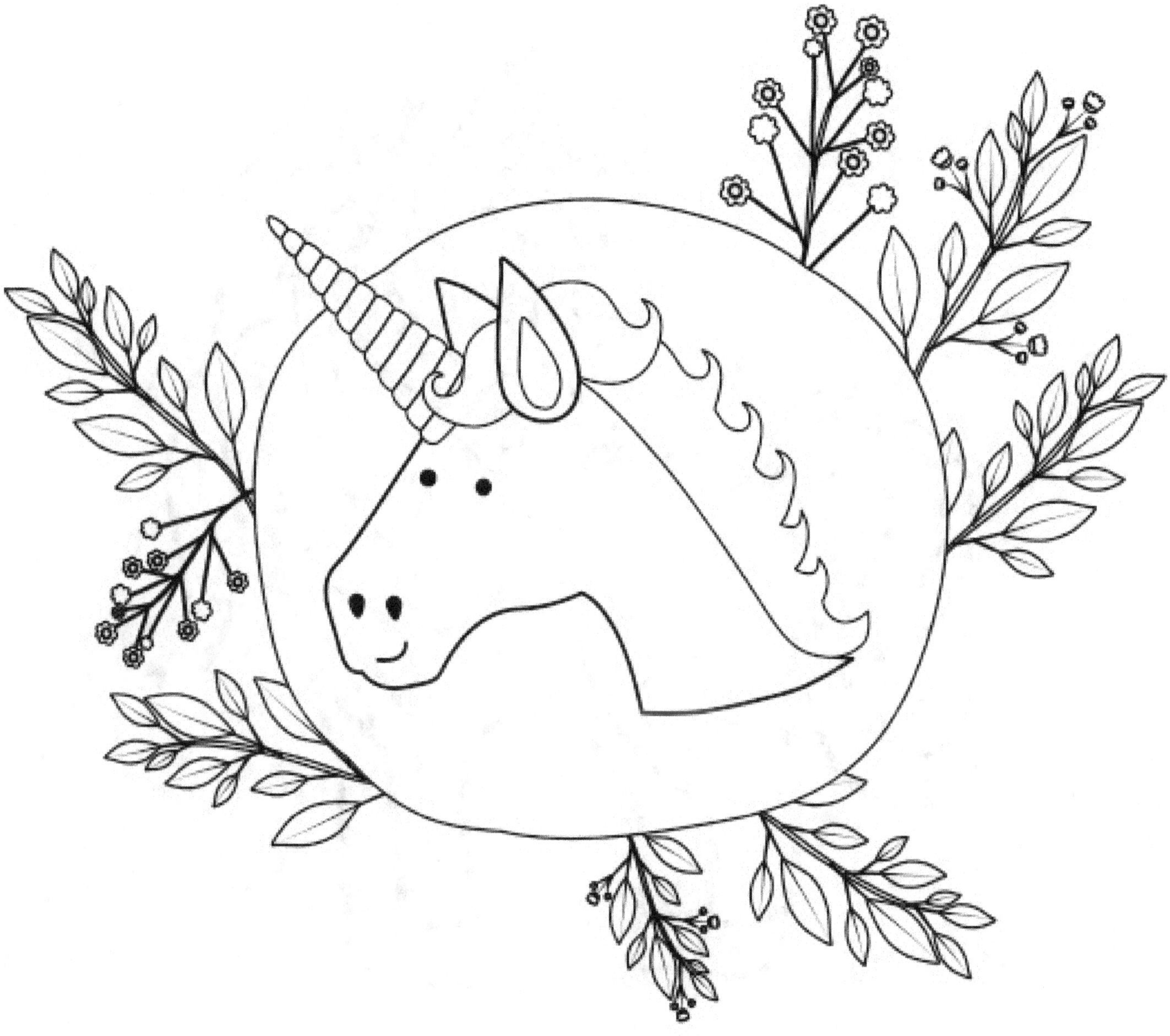

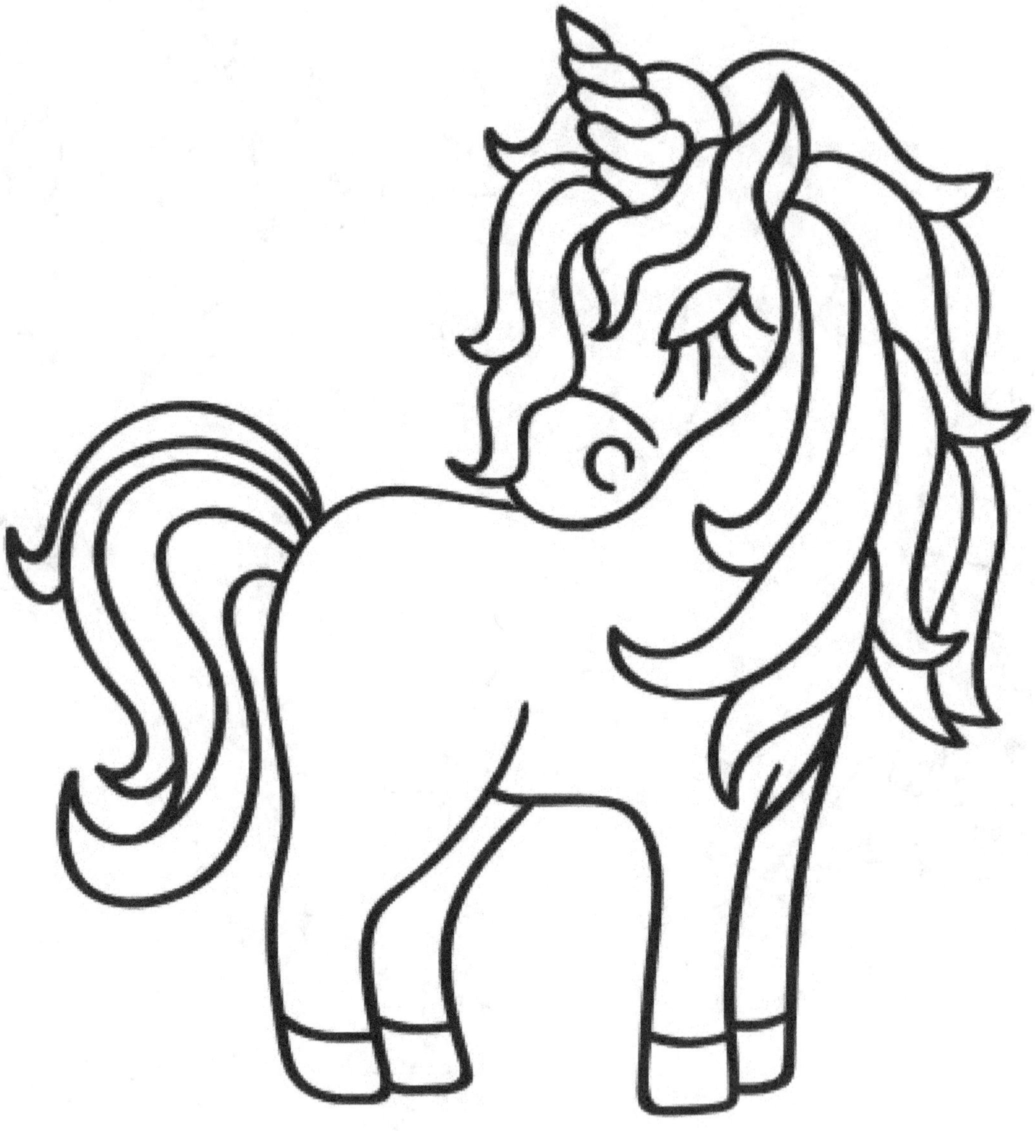

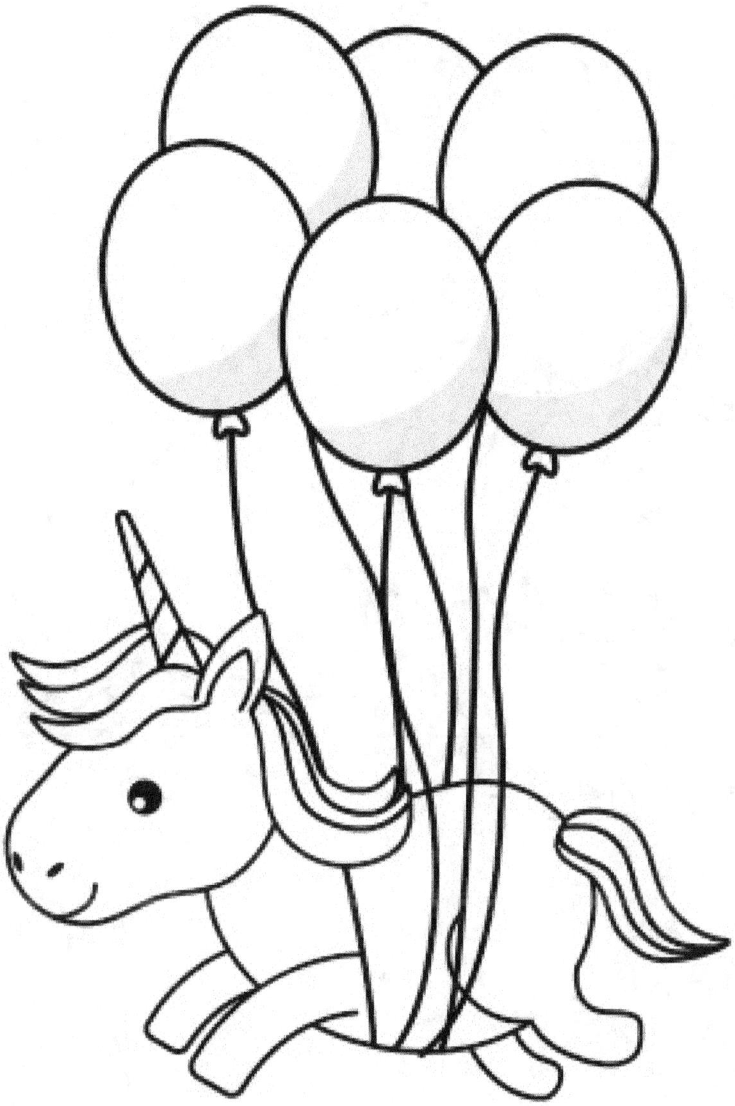

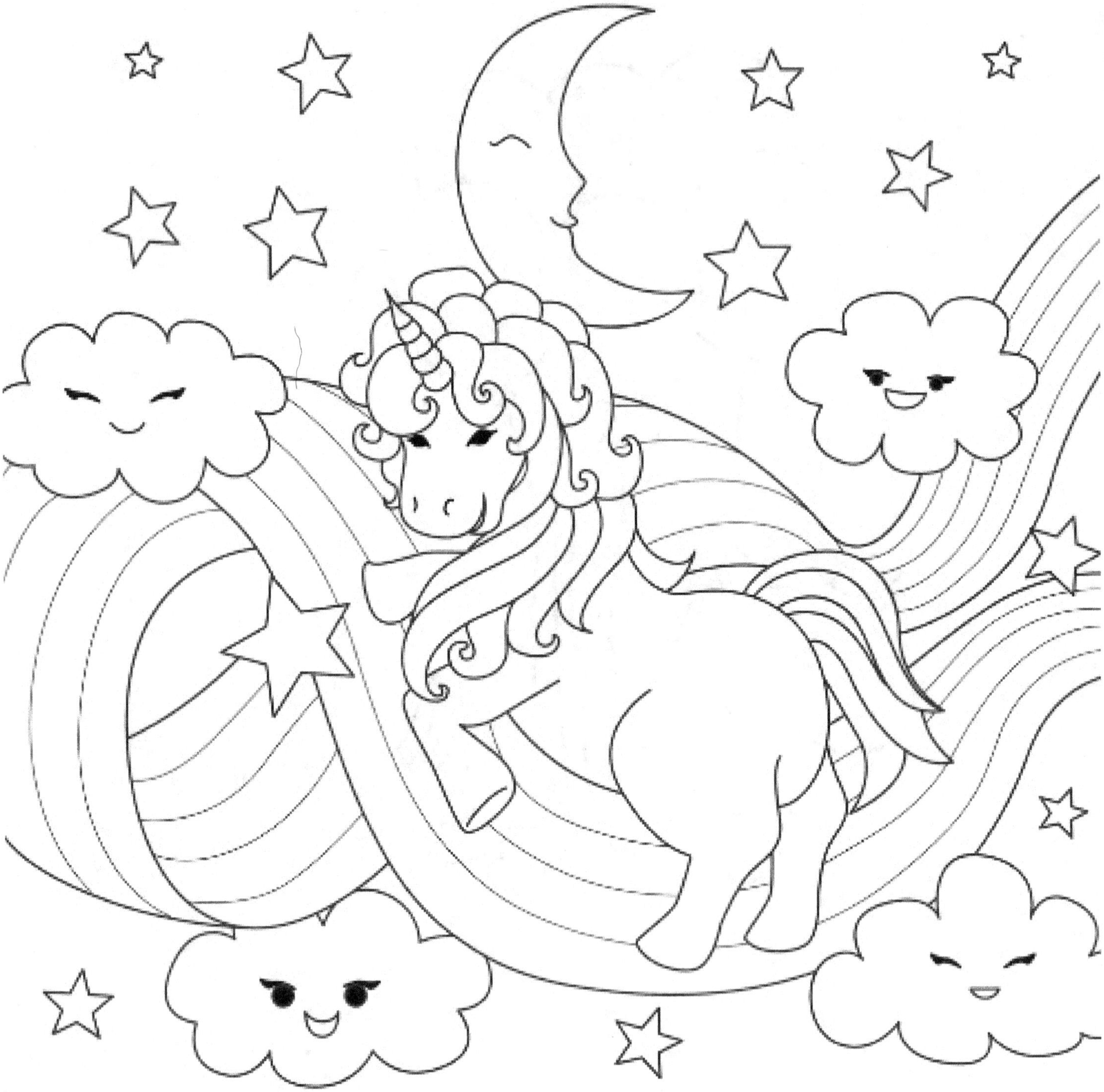

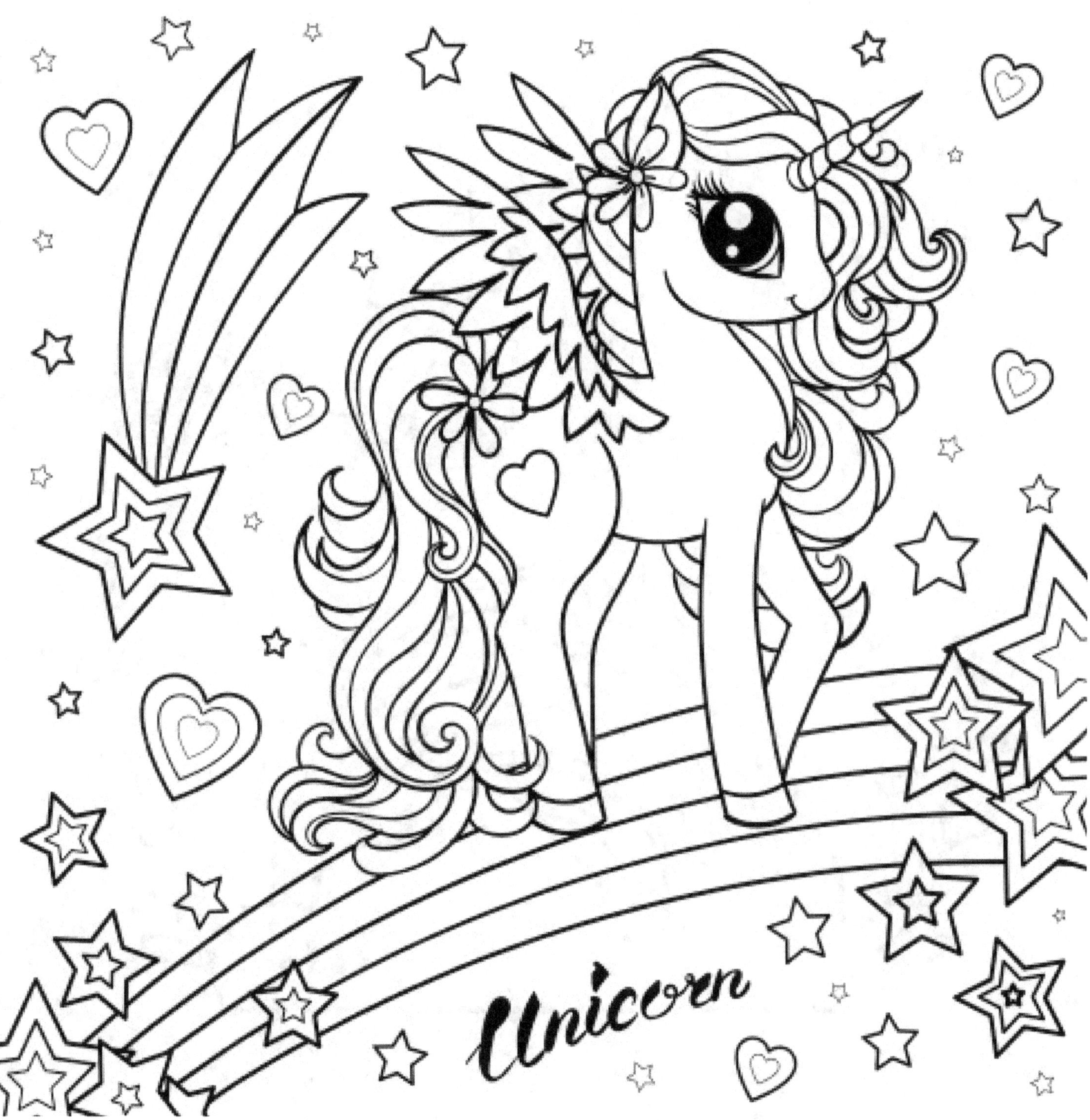
Unicorn

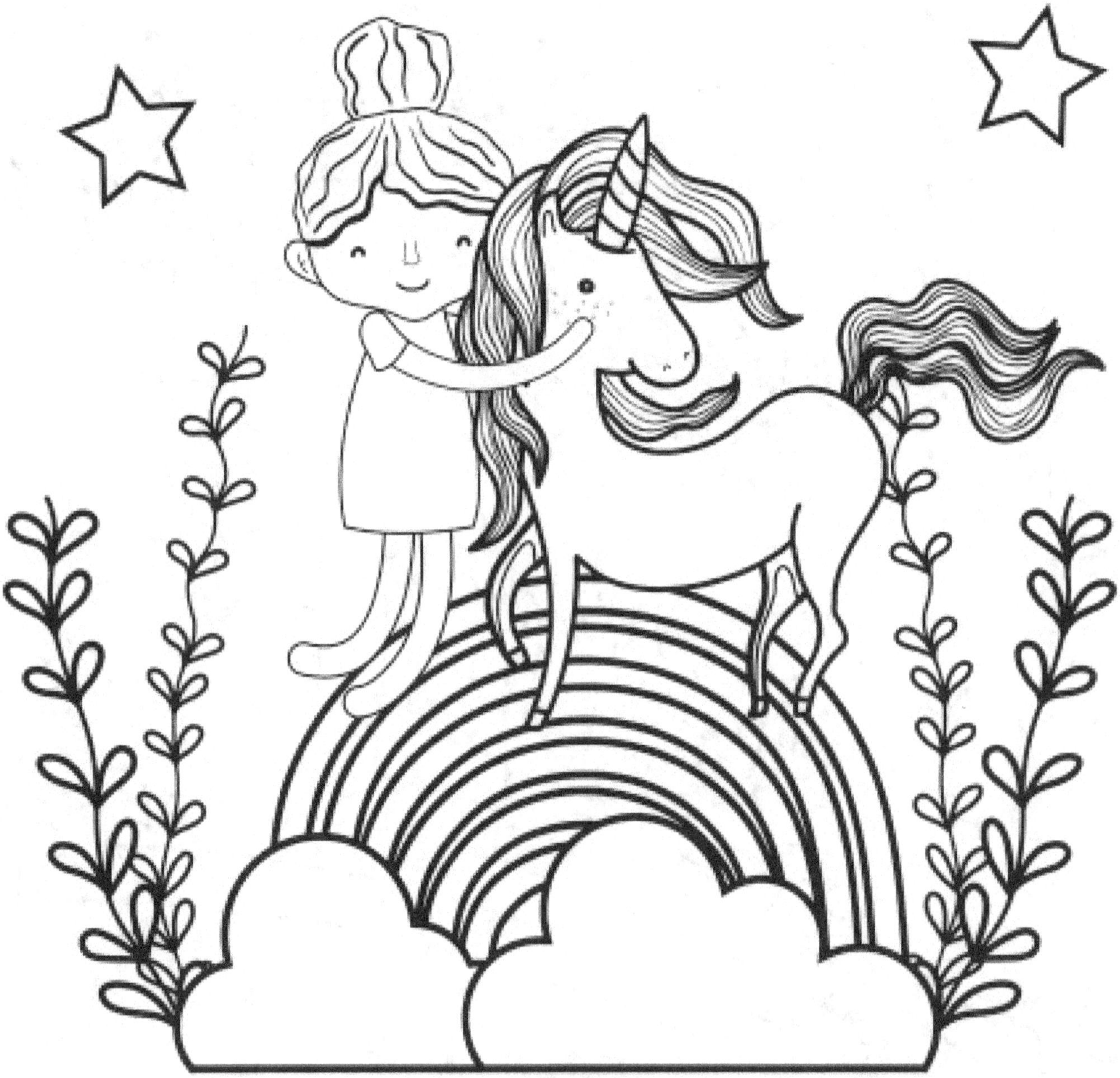

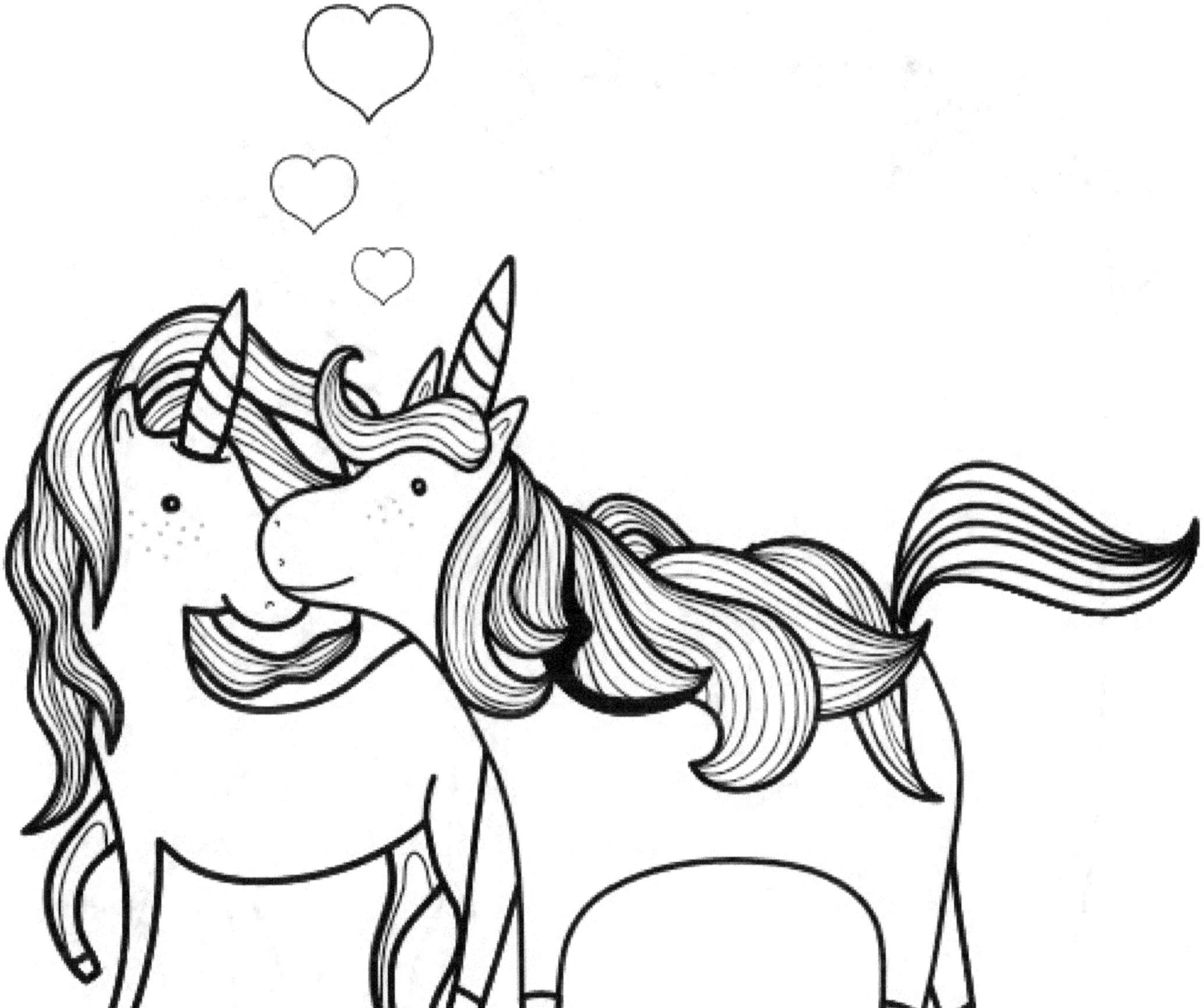

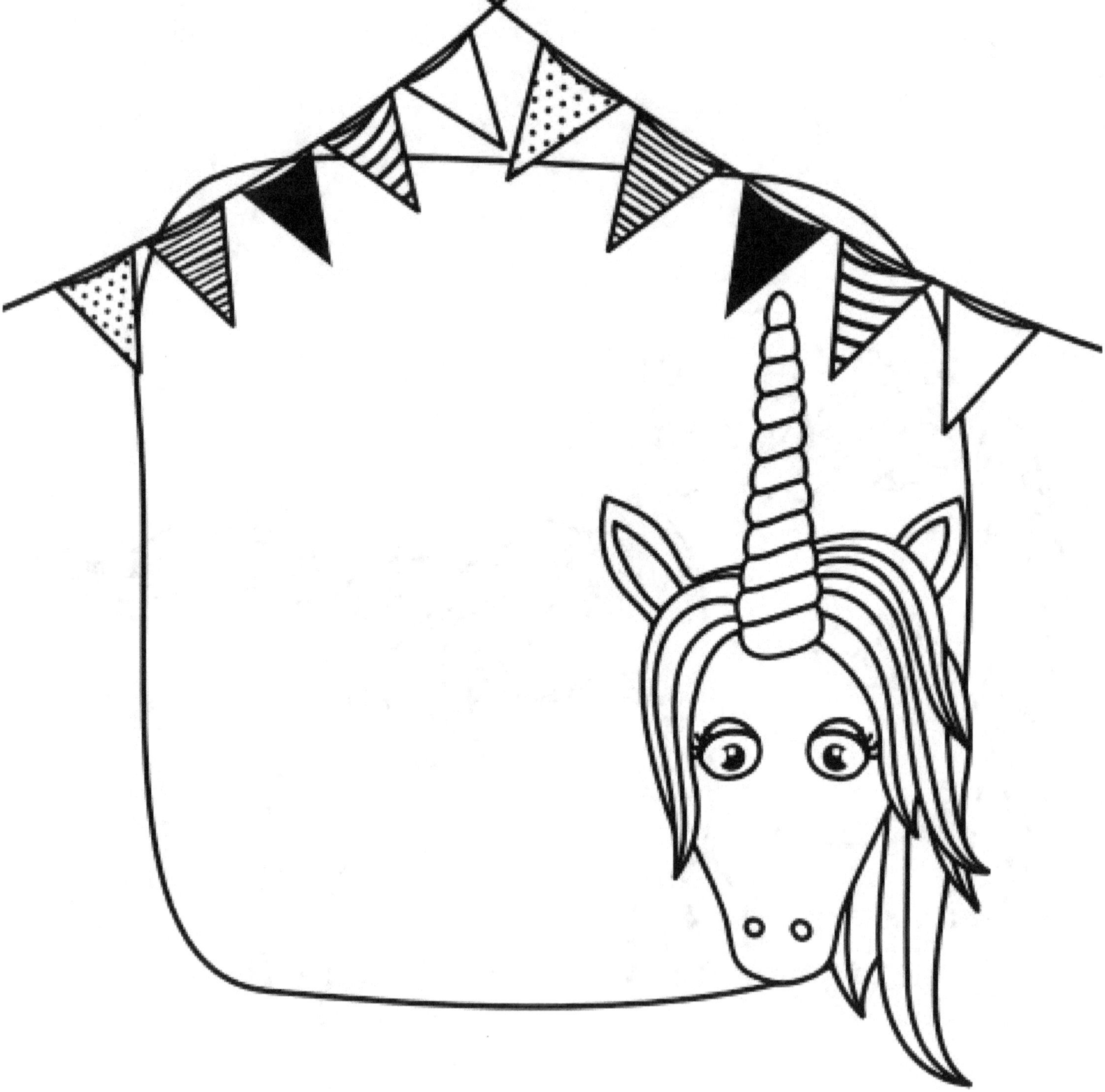

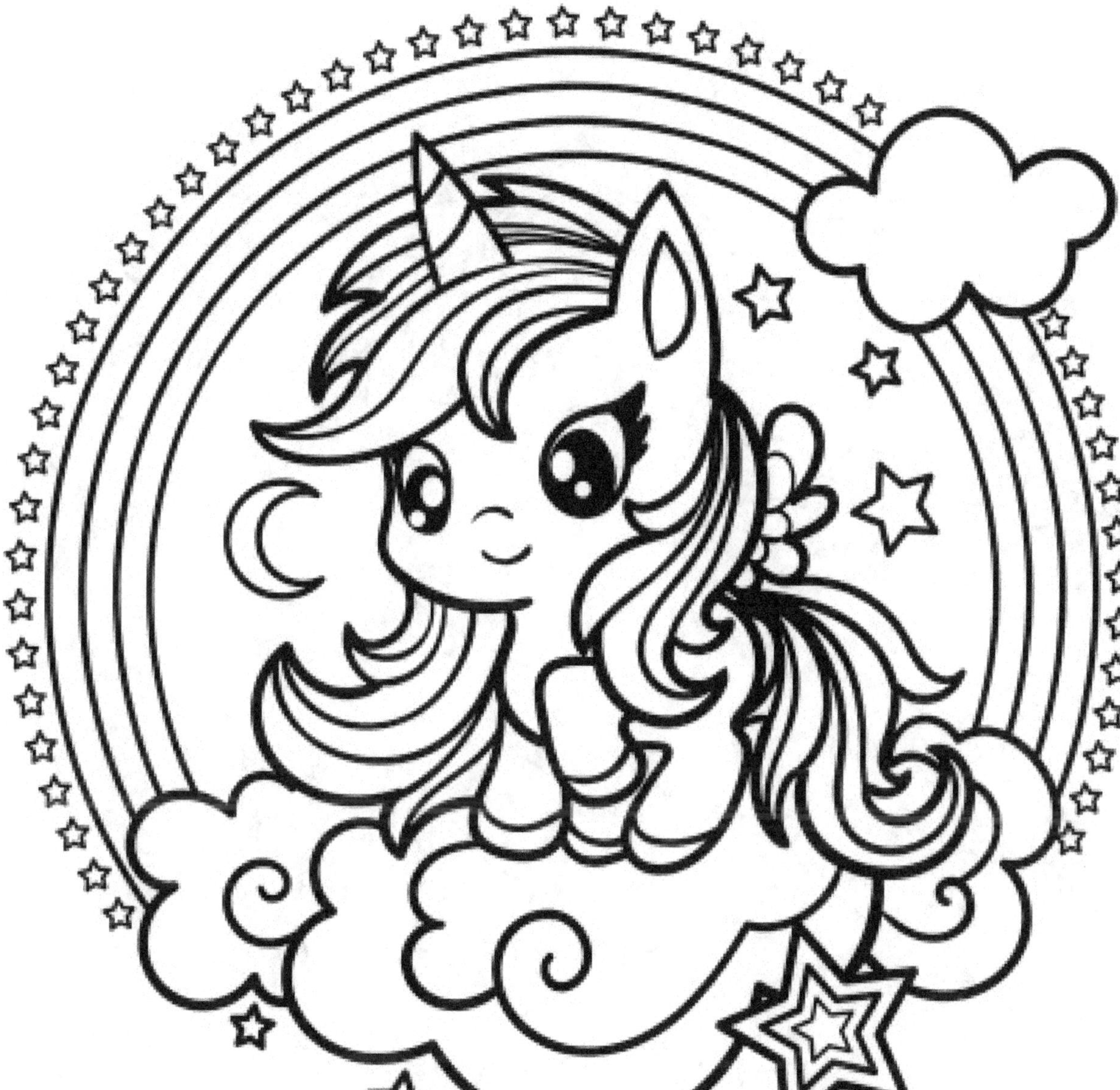

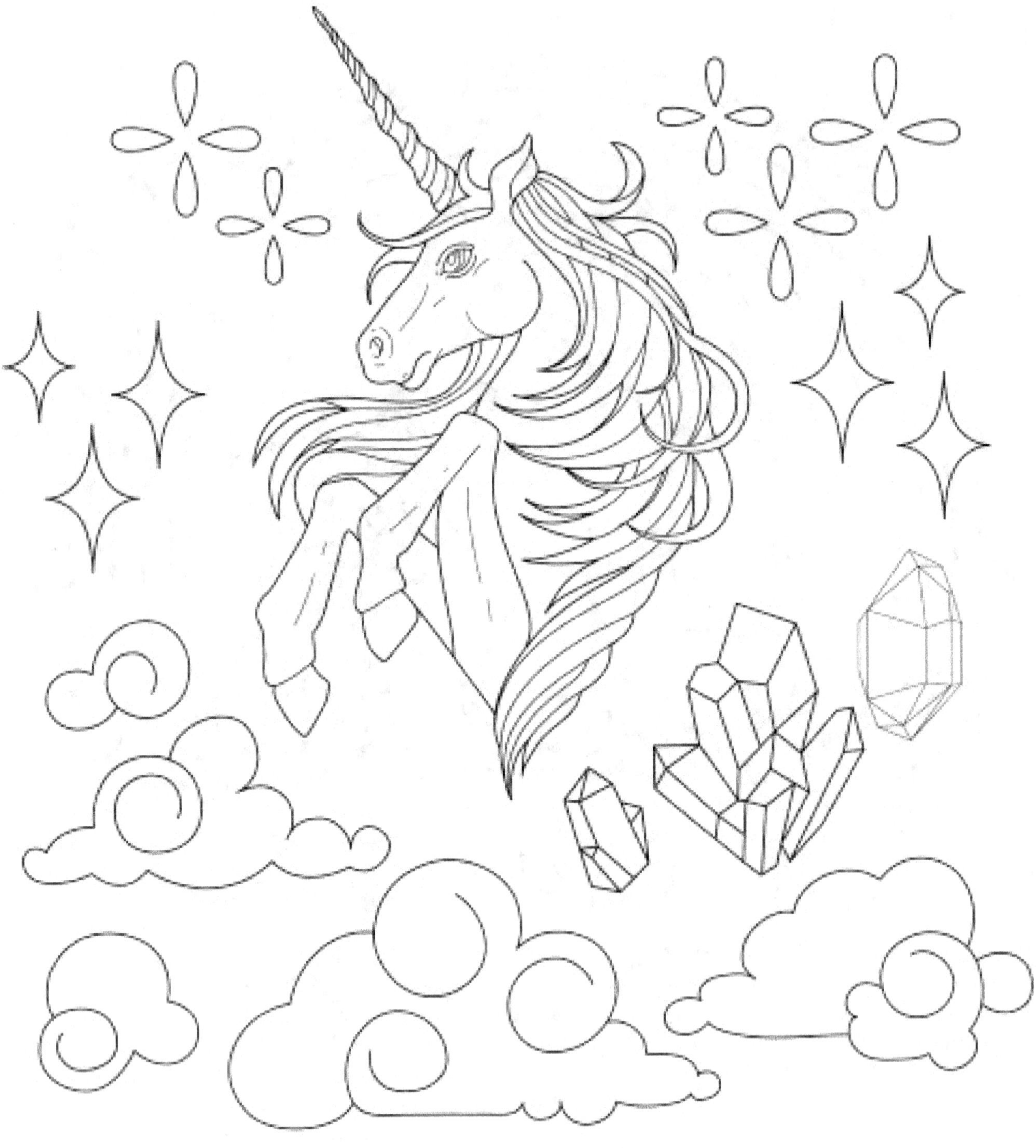

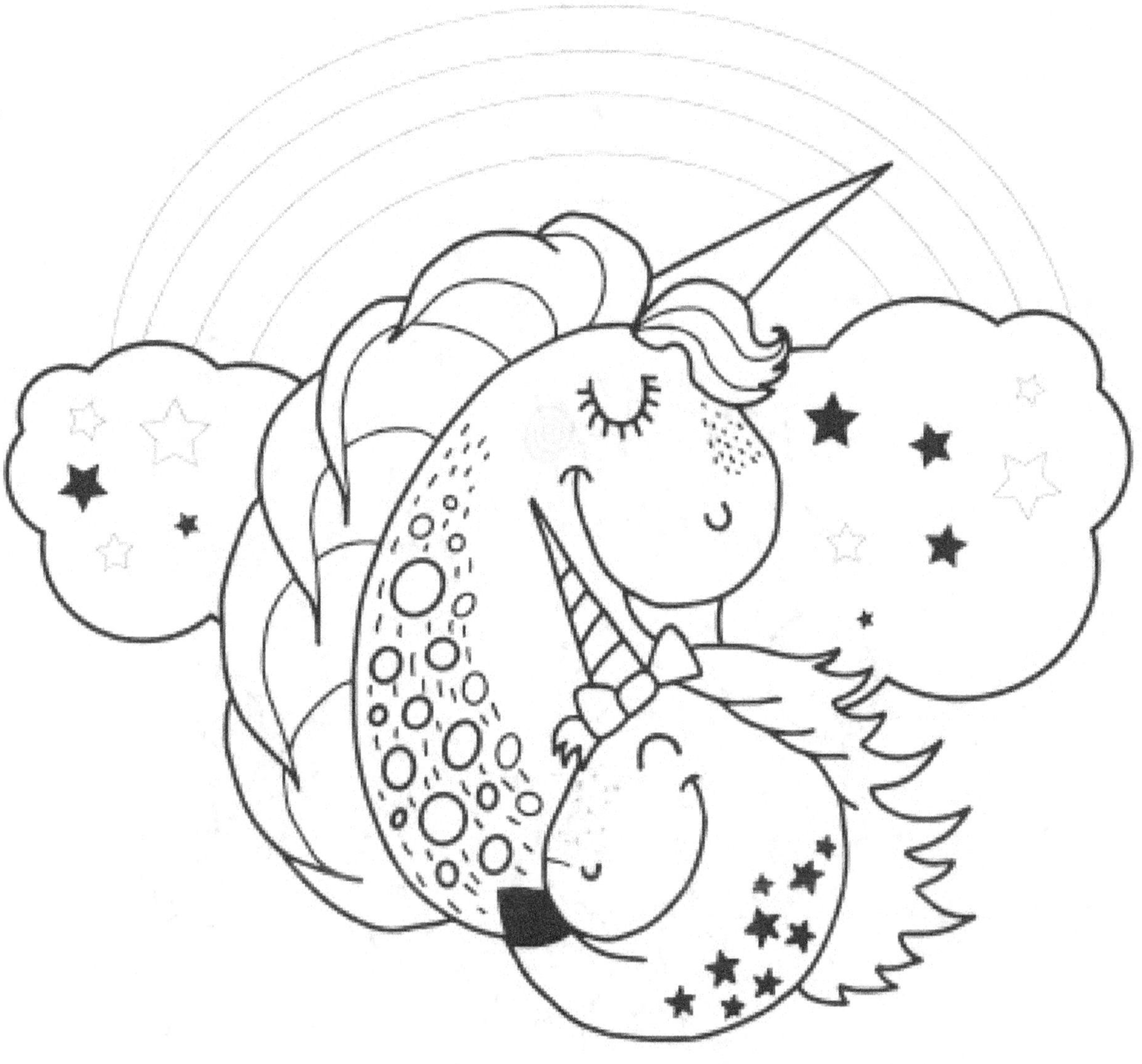

MAGIC

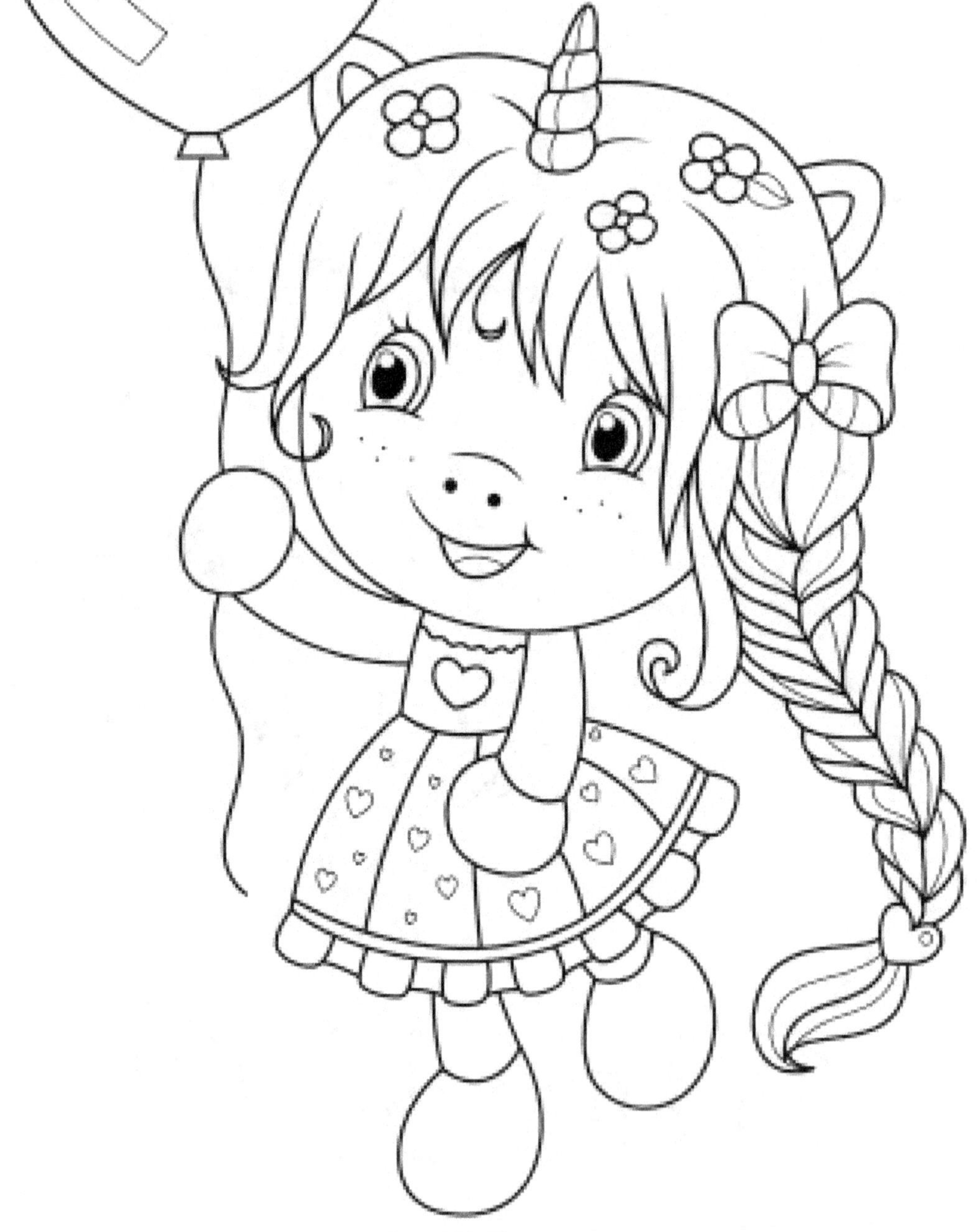

UNICORN

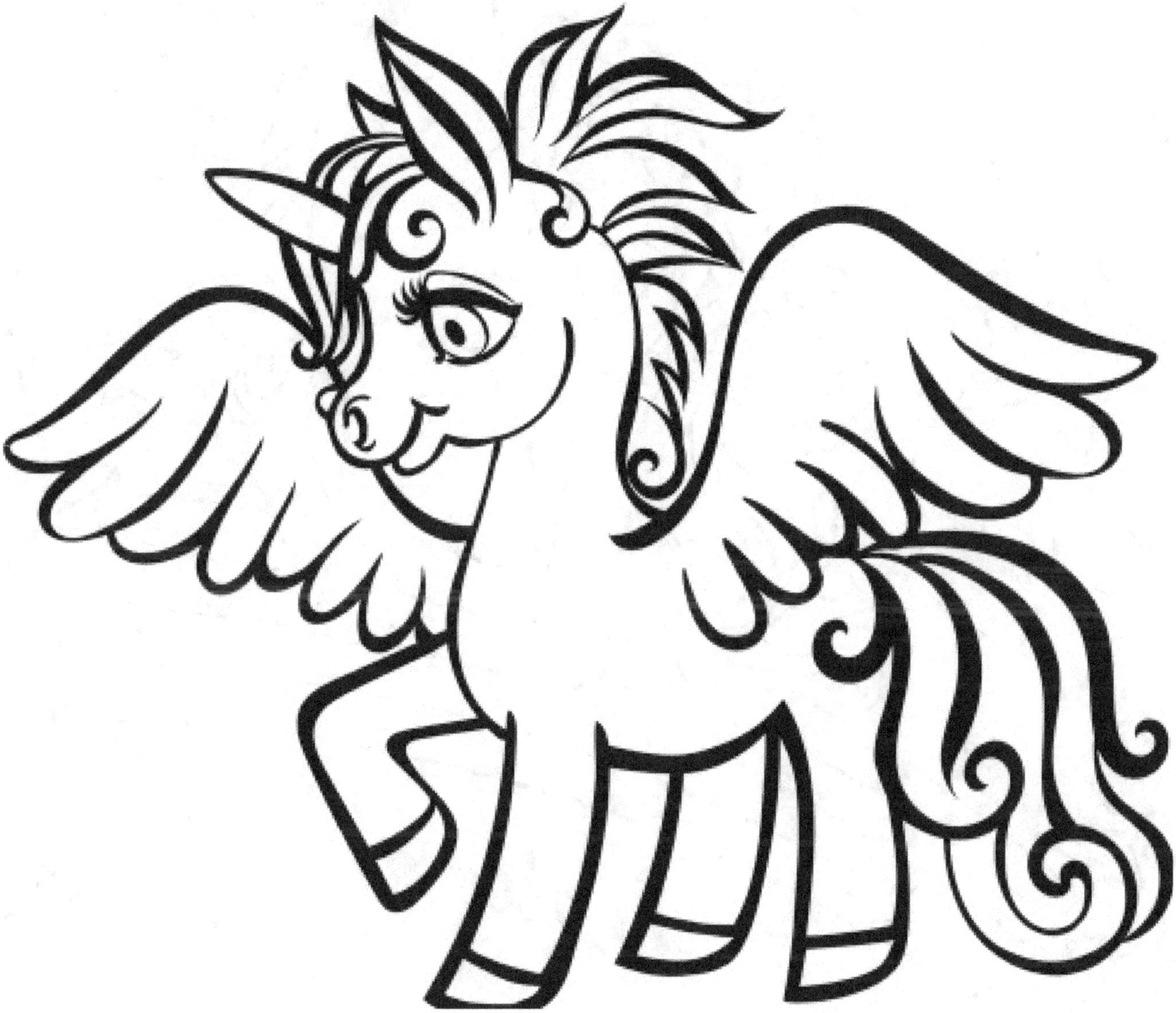

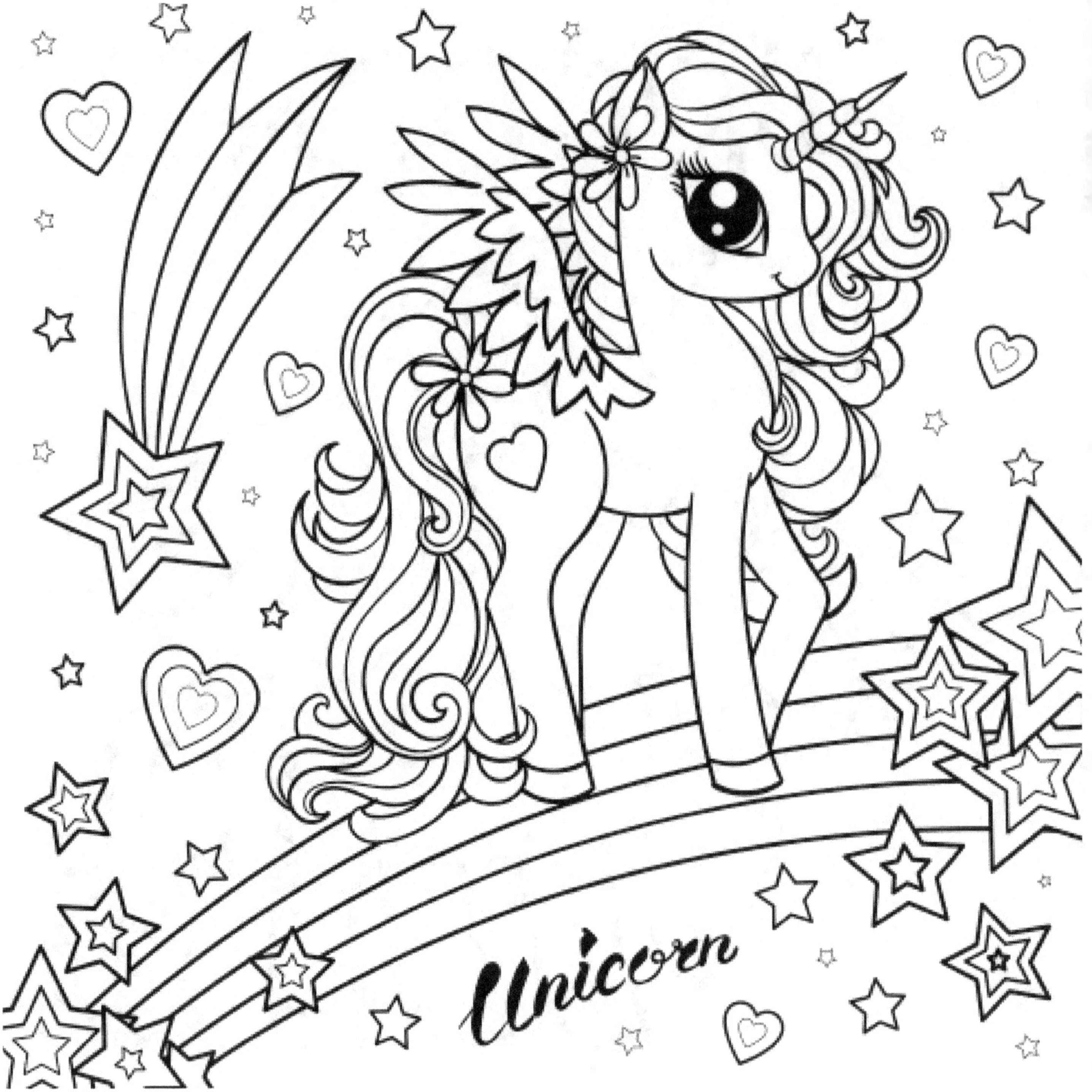
Unicorn

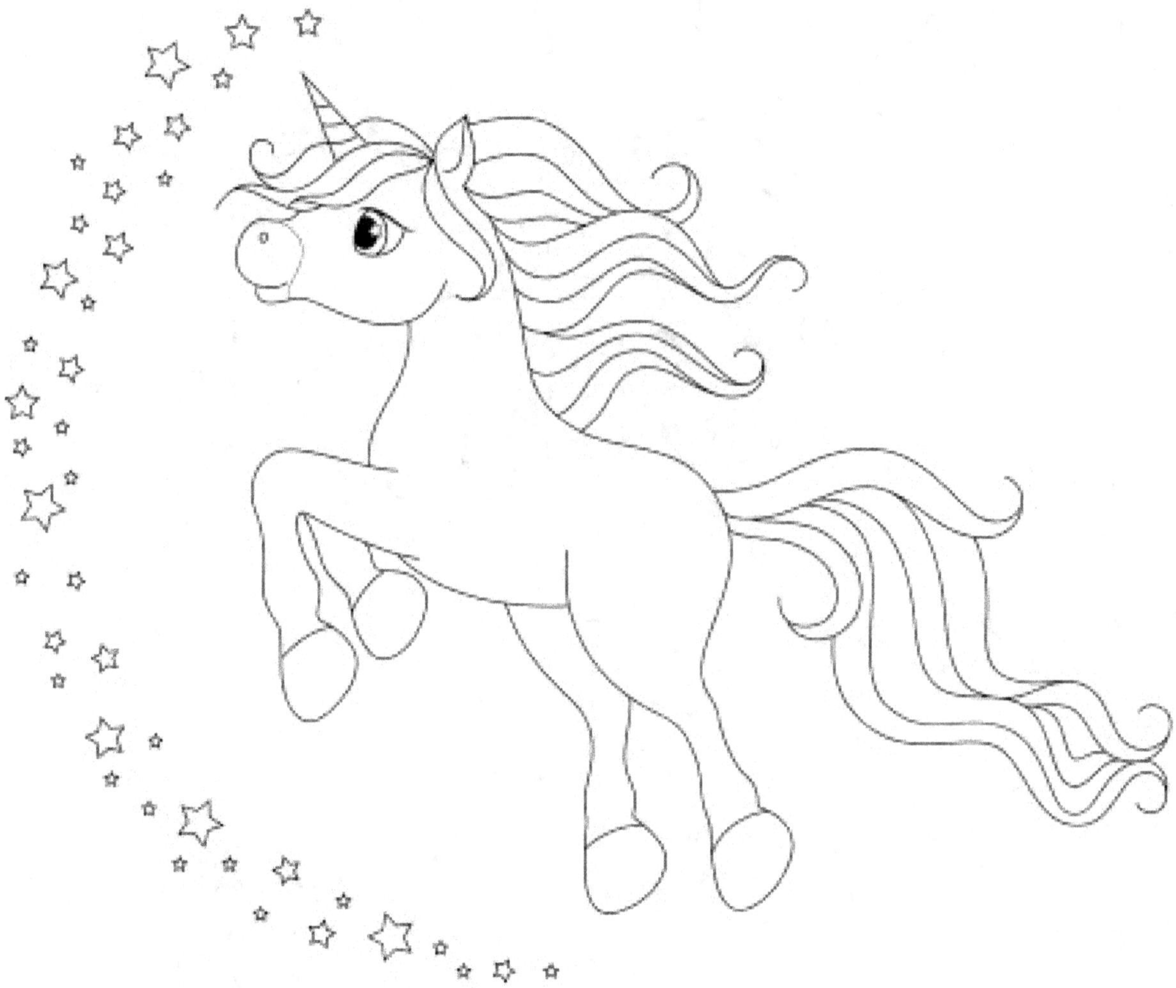

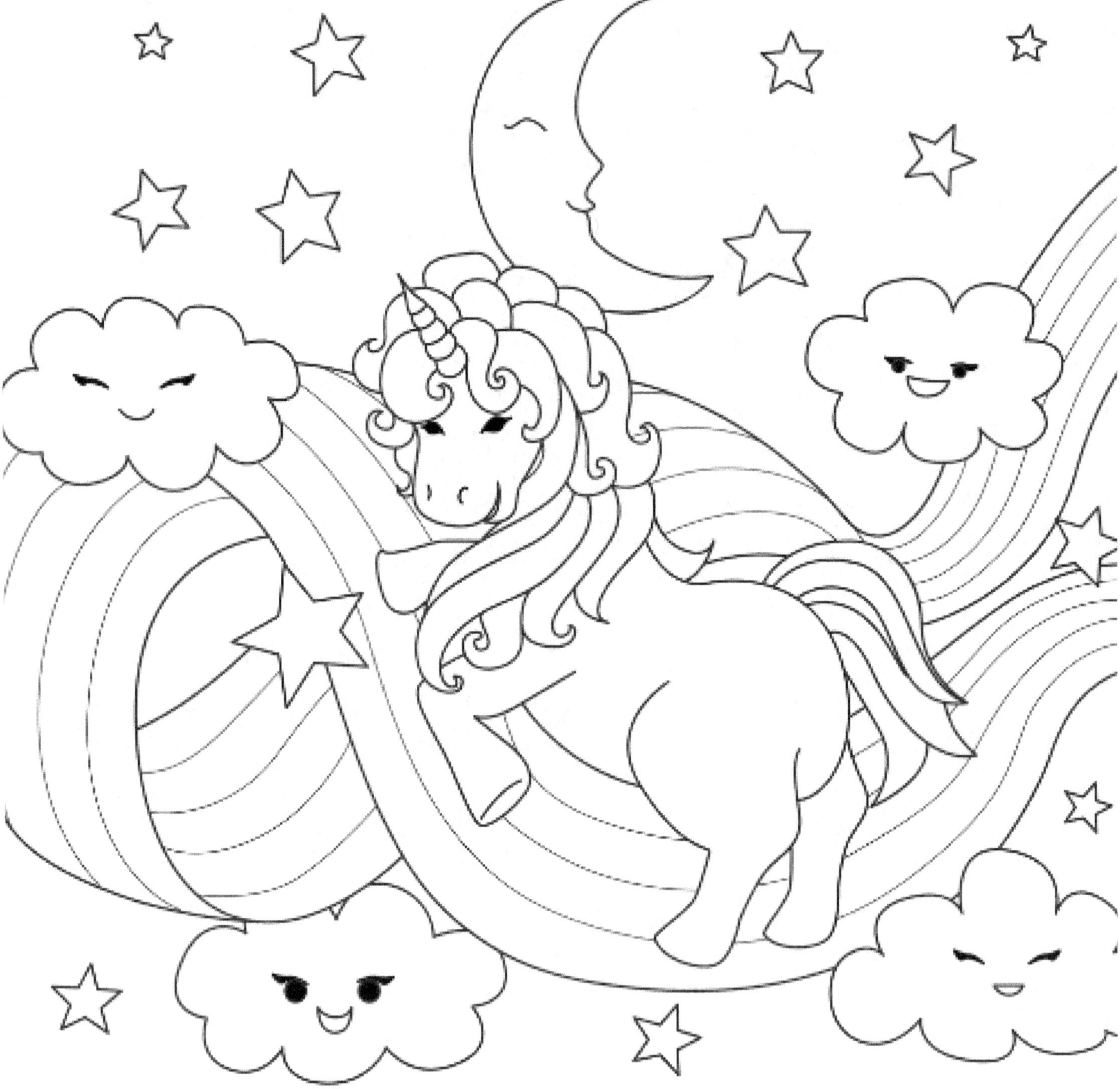

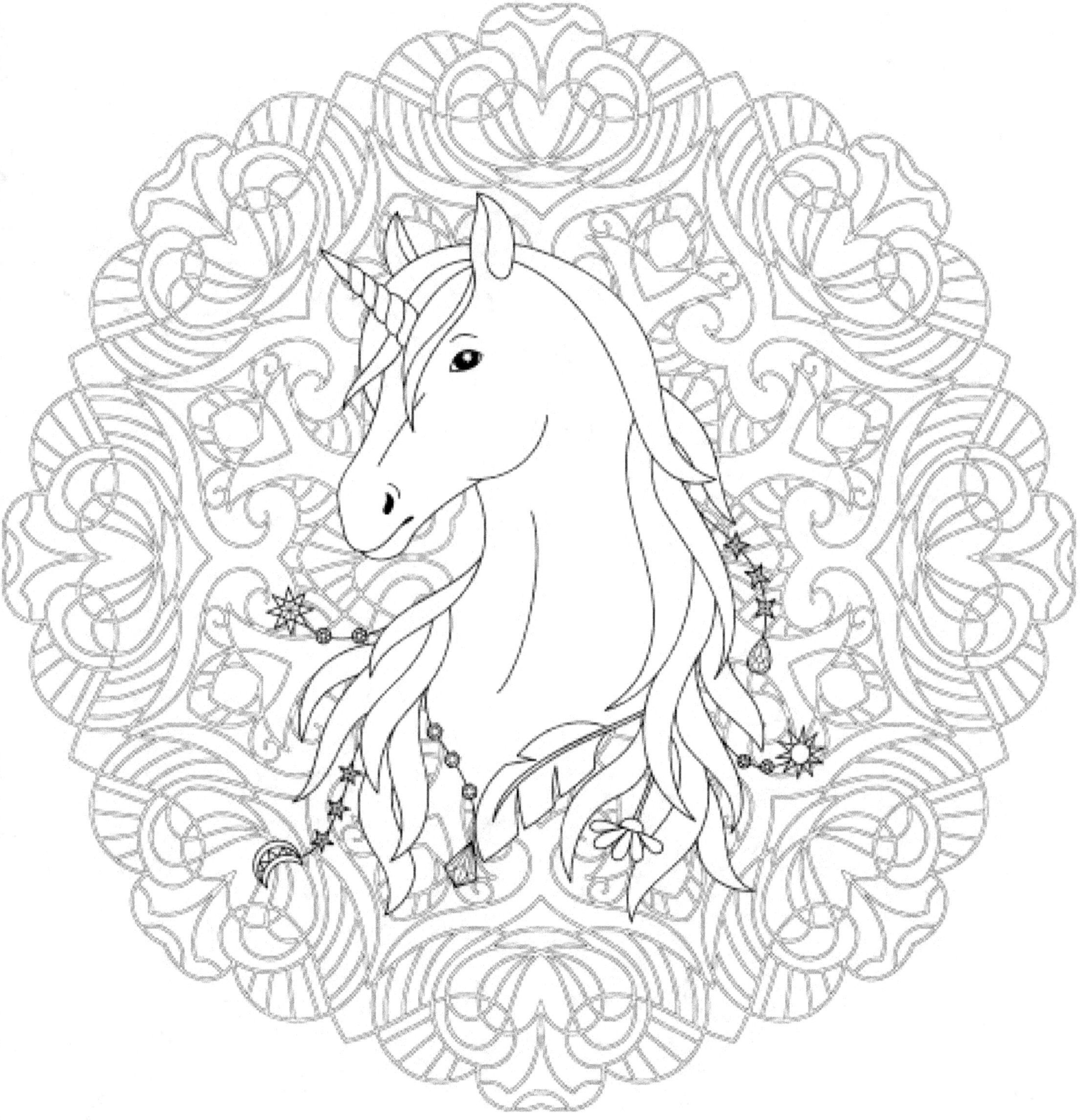

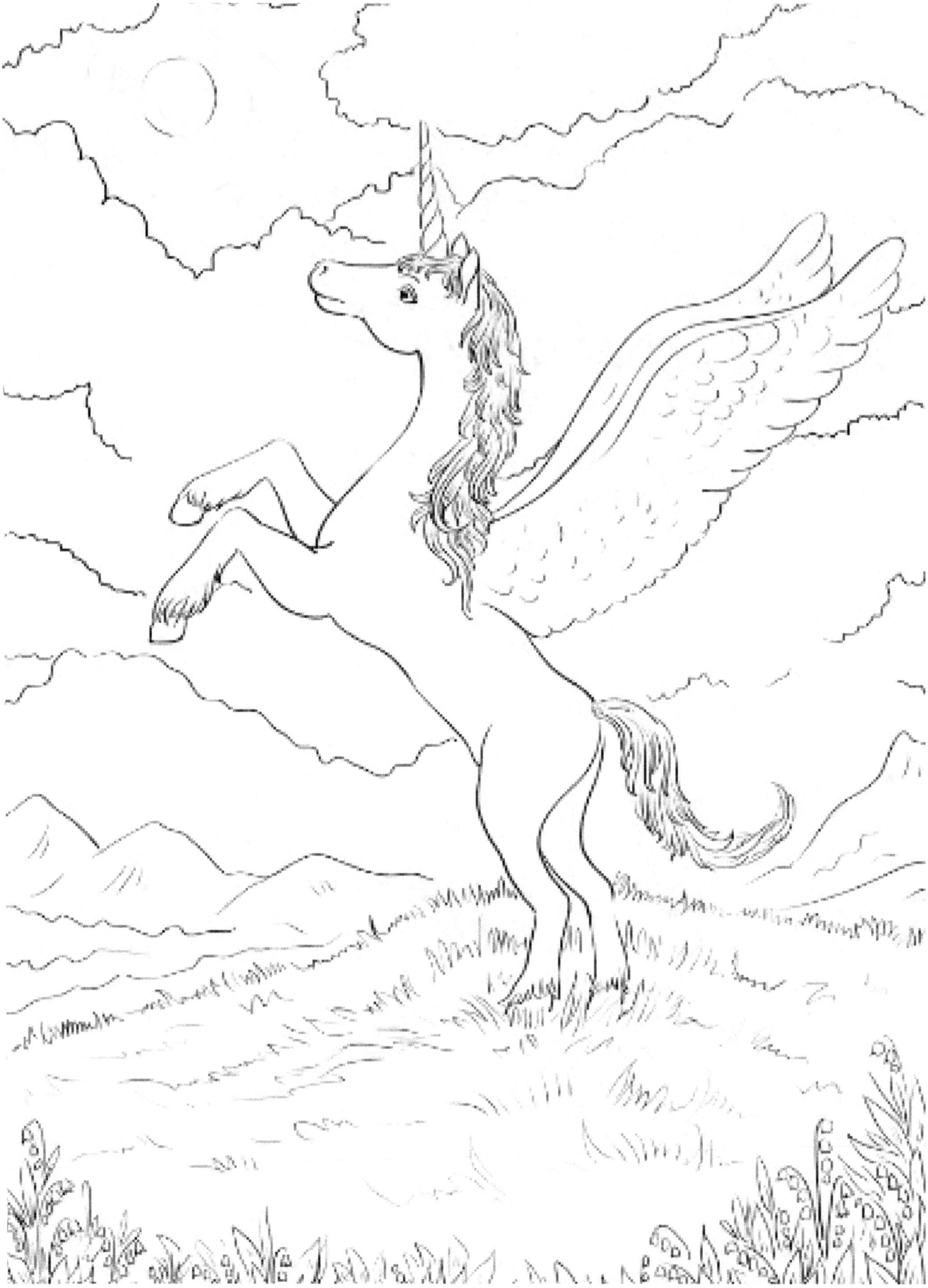

www.ingramcontent.com/pod-product-compliance
Lightning Source LLC
Chambersburg PA
CBHW081458220526
45466CB00008B/2692